M♡mmy Why?

M♡mmy Why?

Stories that Answer Your Child's Toughest Questions

Compilation of previously published books by Destiny Image:

M♡mmy, Why Can't I Watch that TV Show? by Dian Layton, 1995, ISBN 1-56043-148-2

M♡mmy, Why Did Jesus Have to Die? by Dian Layton, 1995, ISBN 1-56043-146-6

M♡mmy, Why Do You Pray That Way? by Dian Layton, 1998, ISBN 0-7684-2005-9

M♡mmy, Why Are People Different Colors? by Barbara Knoll, 1995, ISBN 1-56043-156-3

M♡mmy, Are You Afraid of Monsters? by Barbara Knoll, 1995, ISBN 1-56043-149-0

M♡mmy, Is There an Easter Bunny? by Barbara Knoll, 1996, ISBN 1-56043-173-3

M♡mmy, Is God as Strong as Daddy? by Barbara Knoll, 1995, ISBN 1-56043-150-4

M♡mmy, Why Do We Have Easter? by Lou Yohe, 1996, ISBN 1-56043-172-5

M♡mmy, Why Don't We Celebrate Halloween? by Linda Hacon Winwood, 1992, 1994, 1995, ISBN 1-56043-823-1

Daddy, Are You Santa Claus? by Galen C. Burkholder, 1995, ISBN 1-56043-159-8

M♡mmy, Was Santa Claus Born on Christmas Too? by Barbara Knoll, 1995, ISBN 1-56043-158-X

Daddy, Does God Take a Vacation? by Galen C. Burkholder, 1995, ISBN 1-56043-153-9

Also includes elements from books previously published as:

Colored Eggs for Jesse by Linda Hacon Winwood, 1998 by Winwood Originals, ISBN 0-7684-2205-1

The Two Princesses by Dian Layton, 1987 by Adviser Graphics, Canada, ISBN 0-9693264-0-8 artwork by Al Berg

The Lady and Her City by Dian Layton, artwork by Al Berg

DESTINY IMAGE® PUBLISHERS, INC.
P.O. Box 310, Shippensburg, PA 17257-0310

"Speaking to the Purposes of God for This Generation and for the Generations to Come."

This book and all other Destiny Image, Revival Press, MercyPlace, Fresh Bread, Destiny Image Fiction, and Treasure House books are available at Christian bookstores and distributors worldwide.

For a U.S. bookstore nearest you, call **1-800-722-6774.**

For more information on foreign distributors, call **717-532-3040.**

Or reach us on the Internet: **www.destinyimage.com.**

ISBN 10: 0-7684-2507-7

ISBN 13: 978-0-7684-2507-9

For Worldwide Distribution, Printed in the U.S.A.

1 2 3 4 5 6 7 8 9 10 11 / 17 16 15 14 13 12 11 10

Table of Contents

Introduction

Children ask difficult questions—usually when we least expect them—and they expect answers. Parents, and adults who care for children, need to be prepared to answer their questions using the most reliable resource available—the Bible. After all, the answers to all of life's questions are found in the Scriptures.

Questioning "why" is how children learn about the values and beliefs of their parents, family, and those who love them. Having the answers is the best part of raising young ones because God will honor those who provide the Truth to His children.

As Jesus used stories to illustrate God's perfect answers, this book provides modern-day stories to teach youngsters about the Christian life. The series of books within this edition is offered as an aid in educating children. The presentation is also useful to share with a child, as the illustrations will capture their vivid imaginations and reinforce the lessons learned.

The first in the series was *Mommy, Why Don't We Celebrate Halloween?* which explains why many Christians don't participate in the traditions of this holiday. The success of this book revealed the need for more answers to questions children have about their faith. Other *M♡mmy Why* books were written, one prompted by the publisher's 7-year-old son when he asked about an Easter book.

Three bonus stories, "Colored Eggs for Jesse," "The Two Princesses," and "The Lady and Her City," include lessons that touch the essence of Christian eternal life and the stark reality of mortal life. Tackling the big issues in ways that a child can understand makes the stories ones that will sink deeply into their hearts and seep sweetly into their spirits.

Written by Christian parents who have had first-hand experience answering the tough questions, you will find that the creativity used to sow the seeds of Truth will be an enjoyable exchange of ideas and revelation—for both you and your child.

The next time your son or daughter, niece or nephew, grandchild or neighbor asks you why people are different colors, why you don't watch a popular television show, or why you don't have a jack-o-lantern on your front porch in October, you will have the answer.

Through age-appropriate language and dialogue and based on Scripture, children will learn about:

- Salvation
- Baptism
- Heaven
- Confession
- Faith
- Praying
- Spiritual Death
- Eternal Life
- Redemption
- Omnipresence
- God's Love

Confidently providing assurance and comfort to children asking probing questions to life's most important issues will bring them (and you!) closer to the heavenly Father who yearns for His children to know the answers—His answers.

What youngsters learn at an early age as Truth will stay with them throughout their life, helping mold them into responsible young people who will stand strong for Jesus, their Savior. The Truth in this series of books lays a foundation upon which parents, Sunday school teachers, grandparents, and other loved ones in their lives can build. A solid Christian framework of Truth will protect children when life's inevitable storms begin to swirl around them.

This compilation of stories is meant to bring light and life to your relationship with children. Have fun sharing God's love with them—they will be eternally grateful and you will be eternally blessed.

> *You shall teach them diligently to your children, and shall talk of them when you sit in your house, when you walk by the way, when you lie down, and when you rise up* (Deuteronomy 6:7 NKJV).

Everyday Questions

M♡mmy,
Why Can't I Watch That TV Show?

Dian Layton
Illustrated by Al Berg

Benjamin and Johnathan were very quiet, and their M♡ther realized that she had better check on them. Half an hour earlier they had been watching a video she had chosen for them, but now that the video was over, they were watching a television program. With one look at the screen, their M♡ther picked up the remote control and turned it off.

"M♡mmy!" Ben and Johnathan cried together. "Don't turn off the TV! It's a great show!"

"I don't want you to watch that program, boys," she answered firmly.

"But why not?" Ben demanded.

Their M♡ther folded her arms firmly and shook her head. "Because it is not good for you."

"But, M♡mmy! It's not really bad—it's funny! You see, this one guy is trying to blow up this other guy, and…" Ben tried to convince his M♡ther as she continued to shake her head.

"Do you remember the little rhyme I taught you the other day?" she asked.

"The one about putting a guard at the door of your eyes and ears?"

"Yeah! Let's say it again!" Johnathan said, as he led the way.

> *I'll set a guard at the door of my eyes! (Clap-clap)*
> *I'll set a guard at the door of my ears! (Clap-clap)*
> *I will watch myself and with Wisdom as my guide*
> *I'll be careful what I see and hear! Yeah—*
> *I'll be careful what I see and hear!*
>
> *Jesus, my Master Builder, I want to be a good, strong house!*
> *Jesus, my Master Builder, I want to be a good, strong house!*
> *I want to be a good strong house!*

"Why do I want to be a house?" Ben wondered aloud.

"Well," answered his M♡ther, "the Bible says that you already are a house!"

(See Second Corinthians 5:1.)

Ben looked down at himself and said doubtfully, "I am?"

Johnathan quickly grabbed two videos and held them above Ben's head.

"Here's a roof, Ben!" he giggled.

Their M♡ther laughed, too. "Your body is like a house," she continued, "and the real you lives inside!"

Johnathan giggled. "I've got a me inside of me!"

Their M♡ther laughed again and tickled Johnathan. "Yes, you have a you inside of you! Your body is like a house, and so is your life! You must be very careful about what goes into your house."

"Like what kind of TV shows we watch?" Ben asked his M♡ther.

"Like what kind of TV shows you watch. Listen," she said, pulling both boys to sit beside her on the couch, "I have an idea! I will tell you a story."

"Goody!" Johnathan said happily. He liked stories.

"Once there lived a very unusual little boy who lived in a very unusual little house. Now, the reason the boy was unusual was that he never, ever left his house, and the reason the house was unusual was that it had legs!"

"It had legs?!" Ben and Johnathan echoed together.

"It had legs!" their M♡ther continued. "It was a good, strong house with two main doors. Through one door the boy was able to see things (actually, this door looked like a window with shutters on it), and through the other door he could hear things.

"The boy belonged to a wonderful person named the Master Builder. The Master Builder wanted the boy's house to be built good and strong, and He wanted only good and strong kinds of characters to live in it. The Master Builder gave this responsibility to someone we'll call the Caretaker. The Caretaker trained the boy according to the Master Builder's Instruction Book, and was careful to turn the boy's house in ways that let only good things be seen and heard through the doors.

"Wonderful characters began to live in the little boy's house. They were quite small, but they grew a bit every day. They had names like Wisdom, and Strength,

and Courage, and Truth. The boy loved to run and play with Happiness, and Peace ruled his heart.

"One day, the boy noticed some interesting sights and sounds in the distance. He was very curious—especially when Caretaker quickly shut his doors and turned the house to a different direction. 'What is it that you don't want me to see and hear?' the boy asked his teacher.

"The Caretaker spoke firmly. 'The world where we live is a good world, but there is much evil in it. I turned you and shut your doors to keep wrong things from entering your house.'

"'Oh,' said the boy, as he turned his attention to the Caretaker's lessons. Wisdom and the other fine characters grew as the boy studied the Master Builder's Instruction Book each day.

"As the boy grew older, he realized that he could turn his own house, and that he could open his own doors—without the help of his Caretaker. He was careful to see and listen to only good things; but one day, the boy saw some pictures. The pictures were brightly colored, and they were moving!

"'Hmm,' thought the boy. 'I wonder what this is all about?'

"Just then, Wisdom came and stood beside the boy and told him to shut the door, but the boy argued with Wisdom. 'I'll only watch for a moment,' he said, as he leaned out for a closer look. 'It looks like fun!'

"As soon as the boy leaned past Wisdom, something sneaked into his house. The boy had watched the pictures for several moments, when he realized that what he was seeing was not good. The pictures were of people hurting each other and doing wrong things. It wasn't fun at all. He slammed the door and leaned against it, shivering.

"That night the boy had a frightening dream while he slept. The following nights brought even more frightening dreams. The boy grew irritable and grouchy, and he often spoke roughly to his teacher.

"A strong desire to look again at the pictures kept going through the boy's mind. 'It wasn't really that bad,' he thought. 'Perhaps I should look again…just for a moment…just to make sure.' Wisdom again tried to stop the boy, but he pushed the warnings aside, turned his house and slowly opened the doors. 'Just a little bit,' he reasoned to himself. 'There's no harm in that.'

"Immediately the pictures appeared—bright, colorful, and enticing. What he saw and heard made the boy feel uneasy, but he continued to watch. As he did, something sneaked past him into the house…then something else…and something else. Wisdom shook her head sadly.

"Looking and listening to the pictures became more and more important to the boy. He quit studying the Master Builder's Instruction Book. He hardly ever ran and played with Happiness. He found the lessons of the Caretaker boring and, as soon as he could every day, the boy turned toward the pictures.

"Bad dreams filled the boy's head at night, and he became more and more irritable and grouchy. One day he saw some dark little characters hiding in some of the rooms in his house. They were surrounded by piles of garbage.

"The boy noticed that Wisdom, Truth, Courage, and Happiness were smaller and more distant than they used to be. Strength seemed to have left him, and Peace no longer ruled his heart.

"His Caretaker watched him in concern. 'What have you been watching and listening to?' asked the Caretaker.

"'Nothing,' lied the boy.

"'Where is your Happiness? What happened to Peace?' the Caretaker asked. The boy only shrugged his shoulders.

"'I see Fear in you,' said the Caretaker. 'I also see Disobedience. And, oh dear, I believe Lying is in your house.' The Caretaker paused, then continued, 'Your heart has gotten hard and unfeeling. Unconcern must also be in you.'

"'Fear, Disobedience, Lying, and Unconcern?' echoed the boy. 'But how did they get in?'

"'You must have opened the door to them,' the Caretaker answered.

"The boy hung his head in shame. 'Yes, I suppose I did. I opened my doors to watch and hear some things. Wisdom tried to stop me, but I didn't listen. Oh, what can I do now? How do I get rid of Fear, Disobedience, Lying, and Unconcern?'

"'The Master Builder will help you take them captive—make them prisoners—and throw them out of your house!' responded the Caretaker.

"'How?' asked the boy.

"'Speak to Him and ask His forgiveness; then, in His Name, tell the awful characters to go,' was the answer.

"'Master Builder,' said the boy, 'please forgive me for opening my doors to things that are wrong. Please help me get rid of these awful characters who have entered my house.'

"The boy took a deep breath, then spoke boldly. 'Fear, Disobedience, Lying, and Unconcern, I speak to you in the Name of the Master Builder!'

"Deep within the boy's house the nasty characters looked up in amazement.

"'In the Name of the Master Builder, I take you as prisoners, and I tell you to get out of my house—this minute!' the boy commanded. 'And take all your garbage with you!' he added.

"Immediately Fear, Disobedience, Lying, and Unconcern were tied up in chains; then they disappeared from the house, garbage and all! The boy sighed happily as he felt Strength return, and Peace again ruled his heart.

"'I'll listen to Wisdom, and I'll be more careful from now on,' the boy said to his Caretaker. 'In fact, I think I'll put guards at the doors to protect me—to stop me from seeing and listening to things that I shouldn't.'

"The Caretaker smiled. 'In His Instruction Book, the Master Builder names two very good characters for just such a job. They are Discretion and Understanding;

you can call them Carefulness and Good Sense! Here, I'll show you…It's in Proverbs chapter 2 and verse 11…'

"Together, the boy and his Caretaker looked into the pages of the Master Builder's Instruction Book. As the days and years passed, the boy grew to be a man, and his house was very good and very strong. And that is the end of the story!"

"I don't want any of those bad things in my house, Mom," Johnathan said quietly.

"Me, either!" said Ben.

"Me either!" said their M♡ther. "That's why I told you the story! Now do you understand why you can't watch that TV show you wanted to see?"

The boys nodded together, and Ben smiled at his M♡ther. "Can we look at the Master Builder's Instruction Book, too?" he asked.

"Good idea," said his M♡ther.

"I'll get it!" said Johnathan as he ran to get a Bible.

After they read from the Bible, the M♡ther put her hands on her two sons and prayed, "Jesus, Master Builder, I thank You for giving me these two precious little boys. Thank You for making me their Caretaker. Please help me to train and teach them for You. I thank You that their lives are filled with Wisdom, and Strength, and Courage, and Truth. Thank You that they are Happy, and that Peace rules their hearts. Thank You, too, that Discretion and Understanding guard them and that Your angels are continually watching over them. I pray that they will only look at and listen to things that will make them strong for You, and that they will shut their doors tightly to all evil. Amen."

Ben and Jonathan's M♡ther hugged them tightly as she stood to her feet. "Now, then, let's get your little houses off to the bathroom to wash up for dinner!"

And off they went, saying their little rhyme once again:

> *I'll set a guard at the door of my eyes! (Clap-clap)*
> *I'll set a guard at the door of my ears! (Clap-clap)*
> *I will watch myself and with Wisdom as my guide*
> *I'll be careful what I see and hear! Yeah—*
> *I'll be careful what I see and hear!*
>
> *Jesus, my Master Builder, I want to be a good, strong house!*
> *Jesus, my Master Builder, I want to be a good, strong house!*
> *I want to be a good strong house!*

Hugga Wugga Verses

Here are some verses from the Master Builder's Instruction Book to help you. They are from the Hugga Wugga Version (the author's own), and are fun to memorize! Say them with rhythm and add a few actions to emphasize the words.

"Psalm 101 verse 3—I will set before my eyes no evil thing!"

"Second Corinthians 10 verse 5—Bring every thought captive and make it obey Christ!"

"Hey, don't you know that you're not your own; you were bought with a price—that's right! Therefore glorify God with your body— 1 Corinthians 6, verse 20."

"Look at verse 8 of Philippians 4—the kind of thoughts to let in the door! Whatever is true, whatever is good, whatever is pure, and right; whatever is lovely and worthwhile—keep those thoughts on your mind! Keep *those* thoughts on your mind!"

M♡mmy,
Why Did Jesus Have to Die?

Dian Layton
Illustrated by Al Berg

One day, Ben and his little brother, Johnathan, were looking at a Bible story-book together. Ben was trying to explain the pictures to Johnathan, while their M♡ther looked up from her work with a smile. "This is where Jesus was praying in the garden and all His friends fell asleep—that's what I do sometimes when M♡mmy prays with us at bedtime!"

Johnathan said, "Uh-huh," and nodded while Ben continued turning the pages and telling about each picture, until he came to the one he had been looking for.

"…And this—is when Jesus died on the cross!" Ben announced.

"And those are the bad soldiers, right?" Johnathan interrupted, pointing to the page.

"Yes," nodded Ben. "Those are the bad soldiers."

"Well," the boys' M♡ther said as she walked over to them, "what they did was sure bad, but Jesus loved them anyway—just like He loves us when we do something wrong."

"Jesus could have gotten away from those soldiers anytime He wanted, right M♡m?" asked Ben with confidence.

"That's right, Ben," she nodded. "He could have called thousands of angels to come and get Him." (See Matthew 26:53.) "He could have just left and gone up into Heaven, but He didn't want to. He wanted to die."

"He wanted to die?" wondered Ben. "M♡mmy, why did He want to do that?!"

"He wanted to die for us—for you and me, and for every person who would ever be born. Jesus wanted to take the punishment that we all deserve." Their M♡ther paused thoughtfully, then continued. "Suppose one of you boys were disobedient...what would happen?"

"We'd get disciplined!" Ben said without hesitation.

"That's right," Johnathan nodded. "We'd get disciplined!"

"And suppose..." said their M♡ther, "just suppose...that I said that I would take your discipline for you! Would you still have to take it?" She smiled at their expressions of wonder.

"M♡m," said Johnathan hopefully, "that's a great idea!"

"It is a great idea!" she laughed. "And that's exactly what Jesus did for us. He took our discipline; He took our punishment."

"Punishment for what?" Ben wondered aloud. "What did we do that was so awful that Jesus had to die?"

"Well," she began, as she sat down with her two sons, "it's a long story."

"Goody!" Johnathan said happily. He liked stories.

"Let's see if we can find the pictures in your Bible storybook," their Mother said as she turned to the front of the book. "Yes, here it is…in the very beginning, God made the world. He created a man and a woman whom He loved very much. Their names were Adam and Eve. God put Adam and Eve in a beautiful garden called Eden. It was a wonderful place to live, and there was only one rule. Hmm…Just one rule! Wouldn't it be great if you boys only had to remember one rule?!"

Ben and Johnathan nodded with a sigh. Their Mother gave them an encouraging hug and continued. "God told Adam and Eve that they could eat whatever they wanted…except for one thing: the fruit of the Tree of the Knowledge of Good and Evil. God said that if they ate that fruit, on that day they would die.

"Only one rule…and Adam and Eve broke it. The Bible calls disobedience 'sin.' Adam and Eve looked at the tree (that was their first mistake), and then they ate from it."

Their Mother put one hand under her chin thoughtfully. "Hmm…God said that if they ate that fruit, on that day they would die. Did Adam and Eve die that day?"

Ben and Johnathan nodded and shook their heads at the same time, puzzled. "Yes…uh, no…uh…yes, I think so."

Their Mother nodded. "Yes, they did. Their 'spirit man' died that day, and their bodies began to die."

"That spiritual death was passed on to Adam and Eve's children. Every person born after Adam and Eve, were born as sinners. The Bible says we are all 'dead in trespasses and sins.'" (See Ephesians 2:1.)

"Some people think that if they are very good, they will be able to have eternal life in Heaven. The Bible says that no one is good enough." (See Romans 3:12.) "We can't have eternal life in Heaven because our spirit man is dead! Being good enough can't bring our spirit man to life!"

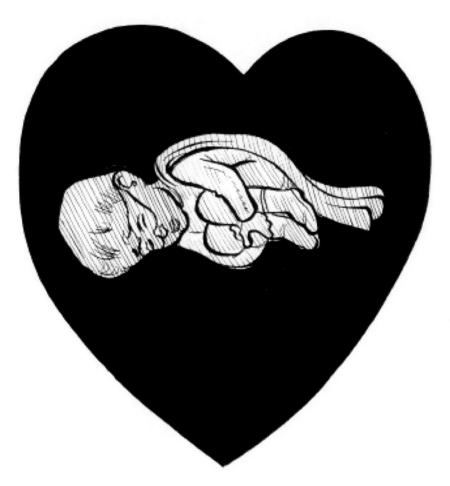

Ben looked up at his M♡ther with worried eyes. "Then how can our spirit man come to life?"

His M♡ther laughed. "Don't worry, Ben! God had a plan! He was not surprised when Adam and Eve disobeyed Him. He knows everything, and He knew they would eat that fruit. No, God was not surprised; in fact, He was ready! Even before He made the world, God had a plan for bringing eternal life back to us.

"The punishment for sin is death. For a long time, the way people's sins were forgiven was by the death of lambs. That's right—innocent lambs that had never done anything wrong. They were killed and their death paid the price; paid the

wages of sin. One of the main times each year that lambs were killed was a special day called 'Passover.'

"But the blood of lambs was just temporary. Lambs could never really pay the price for people's sins. God's plan was to have a person pay the price for what Adam and Eve had done; someone who would take their punishment for them. But that someone would have to be very special! Only someone who had never sinned could pay that price; someone who had never, ever done anything wrong. And the only person who has never done anything wrong…is God Himself!

"And so, God came to visit the world He had created. He put on a disguise, and made Himself look like an ordinary person. The Baby born in a manger that you hear about at Christmas was no ordinary Baby! He was God—making Himself look like one of us—and His name was Jesus, which means 'God with us.'

"Jesus walked on the earth as a man for 33 years. He taught about the Kingdom of God and told wonderful stories about how God loves us and wants us to live.

"The religious leaders hated Jesus. One day a woman who had done some terrible things came to Him. She was very sorry for all that she had done. Jesus said to her, 'I forgive your sins.'

"The religious leaders were so angry when Jesus said things like that! How could He forgive sins?! No one could forgive sins except God! Was He saying that He was God?! They became more and more angry, and planned to kill Jesus.

"The religious leaders were afraid to take Jesus in the daytime because He had too many friends. They planned to be sneaky and take Him at night. One of Jesus' best friends, Judas, showed the soldiers and the religious leaders where to find Him one night when He was praying in a garden.

"They took Jesus and put Him on trial when there was no one around to defend Him. They said, 'You claim to be God; You claim to be King—well, here, wear a robe and crown.' They made fun of Jesus; they pulled at His beard and spit in His face.

"Jesus is God! Anytime He wanted, He could have called thousands of angels to come and take Him away.

"But He didn't.

"It was Passover—the time each year when hundreds of lambs were killed for the people's sins. The Bible says that Jesus is the Lamb of God—slain before the foundation of the world." (See Revelation 13:8.) "It was always God's plan to have Jesus die! In fact, Jesus said, 'No man will take My life from Me; I will lay it down.'" (See John 10:18.)

"They led Jesus away to crucify Him. They put nails into His hands and His feet…and He died on the cross. He died for our sins. He took our punishment. And all we have to do is believe it."

Johnathan looked up at his M♡ther with big tears in his eyes. "I believe it, M♡mmy," he said.

"Me, too," said Ben quietly.

Their M♡ther gently closed the Bible storybook. "That's the last picture in this book, but it's not the end of the story. Three days later, Jesus came back to life! He defeated death, and He is alive forever! He wants people to believe what He did for them…He wants them to receive His gift of eternal life…He wants to make our spirit man come back to life. The Bible calls it being 'born again.'" (See John 3:7.)

"I've been born again, haven't I, Mꙮmmy?" asked Ben.

"Yes, Ben," his Mꙮther said. "Your spirit man came to life when you asked Jesus into your heart two years ago."

"Mꙮmmy!" Johnathan tugged at her arm, "I want my spirit man to get born, too!"

"Okay, John," smiled his Mꙮther. "Let's pray. I'll help you know what to say. You repeat my words, okay?"

"Okay, Mꙮmmy," Johnathan said solemnly as he bowed his head.

His M♡ther prayed: "Lord Jesus…thank You for leaving Heaven and coming down to this world…Thank You for taking my punishment…I believe that You died on the cross…for me…Lord Jesus…please forgive all of my sins…come into my heart…and make my spirit man born again…Please help me to live for You every day…Amen."

Ben hugged his little brother and cried, "Happy birthday, Johnathan's spirit man!"

"Hey, M♡mmy," said Ben, "can I pray, too?"

"Sure, Ben," answered his M♡ther.

And this it what Ben prayed: "Lord Jesus, thank You that You are alive, and You hear us when we talk to You. Thank You that You are always with us, even though we can't see You.

"I pray for every person who ever reads this story. I pray that they will really understand why You died on the cross, and how much You love them. Jesus, please help them say the same prayer that Johnathan did—so their sins can be forgiven, their spirit man can get born again, and they can live with You forever in Heaven! Thanks, Lord! Bye for now!"

M♡mmy,
Why Do You Pray That Way?

(Learning About Speaking in Tongues)
Dian Layton

I heard my M♡ther praying

Just the other day…

It sounded really different—"M♡m,

Why do you pray that way?"

M♡m opened up her Bible

(Where she gets her facts)

And showed me all about it

In the Book of Acts.

Holy Spirit POWER—
"It's coming!" Jesus said.
His disciples waited;
They prayed
and praised
and read.

On the Day of Pentecost
Suddenly—SURPRISE!
A mighty rushing wind blew in
And baptized all those guys!

Bits of fire on each head,

But it did not burn;

And they spoke in languages

That they did not learn!

In Jerusalem that very day
Were folks from all around;
They were shocked and wondered
When they heard the sound!

"They're talking in our languages!
But hey, how can that be?
We're from distant places
And they're from Galilee!"

Well, Peter stood up boldly—
"Listen! I'll explain…."
And Peter preached a sermon
To make the Scriptures plain.

As the people listened,
Their hearts grew soft inside;
They realized their need for God—
"What shall we do?!" they cried.

"Repent! Get baptized," Peter said.
"And then you will receive
This same Holy Spirit
If you'll only just believe."

Well, my M♡m kept on teaching me

'Bout Holy Spirit prayer;

Like when we don't know what to pray,

Spirit words are there!

Languages of angels

Or some earthly land;

We can speak or sing or cry

And God will understand.

Mom showed me in the Bible
(I helped her find the page),
"The promise is for young and old,
No matter what the age!"

She showed me Jude verse 20
Where it says to pray
In the Holy Spirit—
Your faith gets strong that way.

I said to Mom, "I need that!
I need it now, TODAY!
I need the Holy Spirit!"
My Mom said, "Great, then pray."

"Lord! I need Your POWER,
Even though I'm just a kid;
I need Your Holy Spirit
Like Your disciples did!"

My M♡m said, "Son, you've got it!"

"I do?!"

And she said, "Yes!

You asked God, now believe Him,

'Cause He KEEPS His promises!"

So I opened up my mouth real wide,

And words came tumbling out!

It sounded really different—

A strange and happy shout.

I felt a love for Jesus

Like I'd never felt before,

Like a bubbling blanket;

So I prayed in tongues some more…

Well, now I know the reasons
Mommy prays that way;
And now we pray together
Every
single
day!

What Is Praying in Tongues?

"Talk About It Time"

Here are some things that you and your child can discuss, either in one sitting, over a period of time, or as his or her interest indicates. Take time to look up the Scriptures listed, teaching your child to use his or her own Bible. So often we teach children the Bible stories; let's teach them the Scriptures!

1. Have you ever heard someone speaking in tongues? What did you think about it? What did it sound like?

2. Looking back on this "Written in Rhyme" story, the M♡ther opens up her Bible to the Book of Acts. Lets you and I do that right now!

- Acts 1:5,8—Jesus said that "Holy Spirit power" was coming!
- Acts 1:4—The disciples were told to wait. So they did (Acts 1:13-14)!
- Acts 2:1—When the Day of Pentecost came, the disciples were still together waiting. What do you think they did while they waited? Do you think they wondered what was going to happen when the Holy Spirit power arrived? I wonder if any of Jesus' followers got tired of waiting and went home? How would they have felt if they missed it?
- Acts 2:2—"Suddenly." They had waited and waited and now it happened suddenly. It was like God said, "SURPRISE!" Have you ever felt a "mighty rushing wind"? Have you ever felt a wind inside a building where the doors and windows were shut?
- Acts 2:3—FIRE! Look at Matthew 3:11. This was what Jesus had promised!
- Acts 2:4—Why do you think God chose "speaking in tongues" as part of being filled with His Spirit? Something to think about is James chapter 3 where it talks about the tongue being so important. Maybe God wants us to give control of our tongue to Him!

- Acts 2:5-12—When we speak in tongues we might be speaking in some earthly language, or we could be speaking in a language used in Heaven (1 Corinthians 13:1)! God understands what we are saying (1 Corinthians 14:2,14). When we pray in the Spirit, we are praying exactly the right thing (Romans 8:26-27)!
- Acts 2:17,39 (Also Joel 2:28)—The Promise of the Holy Spirit is also for CHILDREN!
- Acts 2:38—Peter told the people how to receive the Holy Spirit.

How to be Filled With the Holy Spirit

Would YOU like to receive the Holy Spirit? You can! The promise is for everyone! The first step is to receive Jesus as your Savior. (See John 3:3-7.) Have you done that? If not, you can right now!

SAMPLE PRAYER: "I ask You, Jesus, to forgive me for all my sins—for all the bad things I've ever done. Today [insert date] I invite You to come into my life, into my heart, and to be my Savior, my heavenly Daddy and my Lord—my Boss—forever. Help me to live for You everyday for the rest of my life! Amen."

Record the date and celebrate this spiritual birthday each year!

God wants you to be a STRONG Christian. He wants you to have His POWER to live for Him. The way to get God's power is to be filled with the Holy Spirit. (Look up Jude 20 and Acts 1:8.)

The Bible says that God will give the Holy Spirit to every person who asks Him (Luke 11:13). When you are filled with the Holy Spirit, you can speak in tongues. You don't have to speak in tongues, but you CAN! In the Bible, when people were filled with the Holy Spirit, they spoke in tongues (Acts 10:44-46; 19:6).

The Holy Spirit is God's GIFT. If someone is giving you a gift, what do you do? You stretch out your hands and take it. Right now, you can stretch out your hands to Jesus and receive His gift for you.

SAMPLE PRAYER: "Lord, I want to be a strong Christian. I want to live the way You want me to live, and I want to be able to pray powerful prayers. I need Your help! I believe the Bible. The Bible says that when I ask You for the Holy Spirit, You will give me the Holy Spirit! So I ask You, Lord, to fill me with Your Holy Spirit right now! Thank You for Your wonderful gift. Amen!"

If you prayed that prayer, CONGRATULATIONS! You are now filled with the Holy Spirit! Now you can speak in tongues! Remember, you don't have to, but you can.

You speak in tongues by faith. You will not understand what you are saying. You simply open your mouth and begin to speak whatever words come out, believing and trusting that God understands, and that it is exactly the right prayer to pray! The more you speak in tongues, the easier it will become. Some people just speak a couple of words at first; others speak a whole bunch. It doesn't matter.

Try it now! Lift up your hands again to the Lord, open your mouth, and begin to speak. You asked God for the Holy Spirit, so you have the Holy Spirit! You can speak in a brand-new language to Him!

When you receive a gift, the person who gave it wouldn't want you to put the gift away and never use it. God wants you to speak in tongues a LOT (1 Corinthians 14:18)! He wants you to use His gift every day.

Speak in tongues during your own prayer time, when you pray with other people, and at church. The Bible says you can even sing in tongues (1 Corinthians 14:15).

Fun Verses to Memorize:

(From the author's own "Hugga-Wugga" Version.) Say them with rhythm and actions!

And YOU shall receive mega-power after the Holy Ghost has come upon you! Acts 1:8; YEAH!

Acts! 2,2,2; Acts! 2,2,2; Acts! 2,2,2

On the Day of Pentecost

Suddenly—SURPRISE!

A mighty rushing wind blew in

And baptized all those guys!

(Flex your muscles in lots of different ways.) Be built up in your most holy faith; pray in the Spirit every day! Jude 20, uh-huh! Jude 20, uh-huh! Jude 20, UH-HUH!

M♡mmy,
Why Are People Different Colors?

Barbara Knoll

Illustrated by Al Berg

"urple!"

"No, red!"

"Red's not unique enough!"

Carlos smiled to himself, then broke into a run. "Hey, you guys! Arguing again?" he asked when he came in sight of the two boys. "How'd you two agree on anything long enough to become friends?"

Jamal and Matt turned to Carlos.

"What do you think?" asked Jamal. "Matt wants the racer to be red—but that's so, so standard!"

"And what's so great about purple?" asked Matt.

"Well, since you asked my opinion," Carlos began with a sly smile, "and since I seem to be the best judge of these things, my vote being the deciding one—"

"Just get on with it! Which color do you want?" broke in Jamal.

"I choose…blue!"

"Oh, no!" groaned Matt. "Now we have a three-way problem."

"Hmm…not necessarily," said Carlos.

"Are you thinking what I'm thinking" asked Jamal.

"Yup. A rainbow racer!" grinned Carlos.

"You mean, paint it up with all three colors?" asked Matt. "Whoever heard of that?"

"Why not?" asked Carlos. "We can add some yellow and green too."

"Well, let's go!" said Jamal. "Here comes the greatest racer-painting team in the history of go-cart racing!"

"At least in the history of go-cart racing in Walnut Grove," agreed Matt.

"Oh well, our cart will be easy to spot as it passes everyone to cross the finish line!"

As they spoke, the trio walked the rest of the way to Carlos' house. "My Dad set the go-cart up on blocks for us in the backyard," said Carlos. "He said we could use his brushes and everything, as long as we clean them up later. And," he added as

they went into the garage, "he said we could use this!" With a flourish, he pointed to a pile of old paint cans.

"What colors are in there?" asked Matt doubtfully.

"Just about anything we could want, it looks like," said Jamal, picking up a few cans. "Here's your red, Matt, and your blue, Carlos. And, of course, my purple!"

"Yeah," nodded Carlos. "There's also some yellow and green and orange, and I know there's some brown and black and white somewhere…"

"It's great of your Dad to let us use these, Carlos," said Matt.

"He said they're all left over from old projects, and we could use whatever we want."

"Yeah? What old project is this particular shade of pink left over from?" asked Jamal, making a face.

"I don't know," shrugged Carlos. "Let's put that in the pile of what we don't want."

Soon the boys were busy planning how to paint the go-cart. They'd been painting awhile when Carlos' Dad came outside.

"You're doing a good job, boys," he said with a smile. "Though it looks like you couldn't decide which color to use."

"Well, that was a problem, but only at first," said Jamal. "It was Carlos' idea to use all the different colors together."

"We're calling it the Roaring Rainbow Racer," added Matt.

"An excellent name," agreed Carlos' Father with a laugh, "especially for such a colorful team as you three make! Have a good time, and try to get most of that paint on the racer!"

As Carlos' Dad left, the boys looked at each other and began to laugh.

"Well, most of the paint's on the car!" said Matt. "We creative types don't have time to be tidy."

"I don't think that's all your Dad meant about the name for the racer being a good one, Carlos," said Jamal thoughtfully. "I mean, look at us. Even without the extra colors we've added, we're still different: white, brown, and black."

Matt smiled. "My little sister, Kara, can't understand that. One time she heard someone say that you're black, Jamal. She asked me about it later. 'But he's brown,' she kept telling me, even after I'd agreed with her. Then when I mentioned that we're white, she looked at me like I was crazy. 'No we're not! We're tan!' she said. Carlos' being brown was all she'd agree with. I wonder why we're all different colors, anyway."

"God likes to make things different colors," said Carlos. "See M♡m's kittens? They're both kittens, sisters even, but one's a yellow tiger and the other's a gray panther."

"Her flowers are the same way," added Jamal, pointing. "Pink, red, and white, but all flowers."

"Once I asked my Mom about it," said Carlos. He smiled. "It wasn't long after I met you, Jamal. Then Matt moved into the neighborhood, too. She said that the different colors tell stories of our ancestors and relatives. There is only one race of humans, even though there are different people groups. We all came from Noah's family, and from Adam and Eve before that. After God mixed up everyone's language and scattered people to live all over the earth, they became separate people groups. And God let people's skins be different colors for a reason. Darker skin

protects against skin cancer, and lighter skin lets people get more vitamin D from the sun."

"I remember!" said Jamal. "We talked about that in science class. The teacher said that dominant, or stronger, characteristics from parents are passed down to their children, and that happens generation after generation. So if some people tended to be darker skinned, and they married other people with that tendency…"

"That's right," agreed Matt. "When the people moved away from each other, they took their skin colors with them. If they married people who looked like them, their children would, too. And in smaller groups, they wouldn't have too many choices of who to marry."

"That's what my M♡m said," Carlos agreed. "She said our skin color can help us to remember where our families are from, and remind us of our heritage. She also said it can remind us of how God cares about us and protects us all the time—even when He plans how we'll look."

Jamal laughed. "Okay, so how does that bright blue skin protect you?"

Carlos grinned at his friend. "Oh, it just keeps me from laughing too hard at you, Mister Purple Face!"

Laughing, the three friends got back to work on the Roaring Rainbow Racer.

Family
Questions

Mᦥmmy, Are You Afraid of Monsters?

Barbara Knoll

Illustrated by Karen Egolf

Cover Illustration by Al Berg

"Mᦥmmy," asked Robbie as he was getting ready for bed, "are you afraid of monsters? Scary ones?"

"Well," said Mᦥmmy, "it's been awhile since I've noticed any. Are you afraid of monsters?"

"Sometimes," said Robbie. "The scary ones."

"Do you know how to get rid of monsters?" asked Mᦥmmy.

"How?"

"Well, you can get out a special gun and shoot marshmallows at it. Or you can pick it up in your loader and cart it away. You can take the garden hose and whoosh juice at it," said Mommy.

"Do you know what else I can do, M♡mmy?"

"What?"

"I could get out my guitar and sing a 'Go Away, Monster' song. Or I could chase him away in my fire engine. Or maybe I could make a scary face and scare him away," said Robbie.

"Let me see your scary face."

So Robbie made his scariest face.

"Oh, Robbie," said Mommy, "please stop being so scary!"

"Okay," said Robbie, and he stopped.

"What if the monster makes a scary face back at you?" asked M♡mmy.

Robbie thought a minute. "I could make a funny face at him, and then he'd make a funny face at me."

"Then what?"

"Then…maybe he wouldn't be so scary anymore."

"Probably not. You know, Robbie," said Mommy, hugging him close, "whenever you get scared, remember that Daddy and I are here to keep you safe. We love you so much! God gave you to us so we could take care of you."

"I know," said Robbie. "And God loves me, too."

"That's right. Father God is always with you. He watches over you and holds you close."

"He does? He holds me? How big are God's arms, Mᴑmmy?"

"They're great big—big enough to hold the whole world. But they're small, too—small enough to cuddle one Robbie."

"How does God cuddle me, M♡mmy?" asked Robbie. "I don't always feel Him."

"A lot of times when God hugs you close to His heart, His arms are just my size. When Daddy and I hug you, He can hug you, too."

"Oh!" said Robbie. "Thank you, Daddy God."

"Mommy?"

"What?"

"Good night."

"Good night."

Dear Parent,

Most children are afraid at one time or another. It is up to us as parents to reassure them of our love and protection, and of God's care for them.

We must also assure them of our acceptance. Although Mommy and Robbie had fun thinking up ways to get rid of the monster, Mommy did not make fun of Robbie for his fears. Sometimes a little imaginative play can help to ease the fears. But we must be careful to regard the fears as real; for to the child, they are.

Praying with the child when he is afraid helps in at least two ways: it will calm the fears, and it will allow him to see that Jesus does care for him and does answer our prayers. As you hold or rock your child, remind him that Father God also holds him close in His heart.

Another source of help lies in Scripture. Even very young children can memorize Scripture verses, especially if they are simplified, set to a rhythm, or made into a song. Some verses that might help a fearful child include the following (most have been paraphrased to simplify them for children):

"When I am afraid, I will trust in God" (Psalm 56:3).

"Jesus said, 'I will never, ever leave you by yourself'" (Hebrews 13:5).

"The Lord is on my side; I will not fear!" (Psalm 118:6a)

"Be strong and courageous! The Lord your God is with you wherever you go" (Joshua 1:9).

"The Lord is my Light and my Salvation; whom shall I fear? The Lord is my Strength, the Strength of my life; of whom shall I be afraid?" (Psalm 27:1)

"Behold, God is my Salvation, I will trust and not be afraid; for the Lord God is my Strength and my Song, and He has become my Salvation" (Isaiah 12:2).

"You, O God, are a shield of protection about me! You are glorious, the One who lifts my head!" (Psalm 3:3)

Obviously there are many more Scriptures that could be used; these are just a few that have helped our family. Numerous examples can also be found in Scripture of the Lord Jesus saying, "Be not afraid!" Remind your child that Jesus does not want him to fear, but to trust in His protection and love.

M♡mmy,
Is God as Strong as Daddy?

Barbara Knoll
Illustrated by Al Berg

Robby was sitting on a high branch of the big tree behind his house when Daddy came out to find him.

"What are you doing, Robby?" asked Daddy.

"I'm flying on my rocket," Robby answered. "We're almost to Mars!"

"We?" asked Daddy.

"I'm pretending Josiah is up here, too," said Robby.

"Well, sometimes a little brother can come along," said Daddy. "But right now, we have something that only big boys can help with."

"Is it time to help Susan move?"

"Yes, it is. Come on down, and let's go!"

Robby started to climb down the tree. Suddenly his foot slipped! He almost lost his grip, but at once Daddy was right there to catch him.

"Careful, Son. We don't need any accidents. Just let go of the tree now." As Robby let go he dropped down right into Daddy's arms.

"Thank you, Daddy. You're strong! I'll be as strong as you!" said Robby.

"You sure will!" Daddy smiled as he let Robby down to the ground. Soon they were on their way to help Susan move to her new home.

When they got to the new house, they found that lots of other friends from the church were already there to help. Daddy made a pile of smaller things outside the moving van for Robby to carry in. "Be careful," he said, "and don't get in the way of the men moving furniture."

Robby had soon brought in the things in his pile. Then he watched the men for a while. He saw them carrying in the heavy things—a sofa, a refrigerator, a large table, a desk. There seemed to be no end to all the things that needed to be brought into the house. Robby saw that his Daddy helped to carry many of the biggest pieces. Then he noticed that a few more boxes were outside of the truck. Maybe they were waiting for him.

Robby went over and began to lift a box. At least, he tried. What was wrong? The box wasn't all that big, but he couldn't pick it up to carry it.

Then Daddy saw him. Laughing, he came over and picked up the box. "Look, Robby. Do you see the label? 'Books.' That's what makes this box so heavy—it's full of books."

"It's too heavy for me to lift," said Robby. "But you're really strong!"

Daddy just smiled and kept on moving boxes and furniture, while Robby helped Susan unpack. Finally, everything was moved in, and Daddy and Robby went home. Mﬀmmy and Josiah were on the front porch when they returned. "Up from

your nap, are you?" Daddy said to little Josiah. Then he lifted him up and swung him around a bit before giving him a big, Daddy-sized hug.

Later that night, while Robby was getting ready for bed, he said, "Mommy, Daddy is very strong. Today he caught me when I dropped from the tree. He

moved very heavy boxes and things at Susan's house. And he can swing Josiah around to make him laugh."

"Yes," said Mommy, "Daddy has a very strong body. But he's strong in other ways, too."

"What other ways?" asked Robby.

"Remember when you cut your leg and had to get stitches? Who stayed with you, held you, and prayed with you?"

"Daddy did."

"That's right. That took a different kind of strength. And who comforted you when your pet turtle left the yard and ran away?"

"Daddy did. Is that a kind of strength, too?"

"Yes, it is. Daddy has the kind of strength that lets us lean on him when we're hurting, or when we're afraid, or when we just need to know that we're loved."

"Mommy, I was wondering," said Robby. "Is God as strong as Daddy?"

Mommy smiled. "Well, Daddy is very strong. But I'll tell you a secret. God is even stronger!"

"How strong is God?"

"He is so strong that He made all the world," Mommy answered. "The Bible says that He laid the foundation of the earth. He is strong enough to make the ocean go where He wants it to, and He sets the paths of the waves of the sea. He guides the stars, and the rains and snow come at His command.

"God is stronger than fears and sicknesses. Do you remember all the stories in the Bible of how Jesus healed many people and took away their fears? He can do that because He is God, and He's stronger than those things. Daddy is very strong, but he's not as strong as God."

"I guess not," answered Robby. "What else does God do?"

"When you were smaller, I used to carry you a lot, as I carry Josiah now. I don't do that anymore. Do you know why?"

"I grew! I got too big for you to carry."

"That's right. Someday Josiah will be too big for me to carry as well. But that will never happen with God. Father God is strong enough to hold you and carry you all your life, no matter how big you get. And He always will."

"Why?" asked Robby.

"Because one of the very strongest things about God is not His muscles—it's His love. God's love is stronger than all our fears, than anything that could happen to us, and than anything we could do. It is strong enough to keep us and to hold us all our lives, and forever.

"Since God lives in the hearts of those who want Him to, His love and His strength live in us, too. That way we can fulfill our destiny, or do what God has planned for our lives. Jesus living in us takes away our fears and gives us His ability. Many times the Bible says that God is our strength."

"Wow! So God, who is so strong, lives in me, and then He makes me strong?"

"That's right!"

"But I don't feel very strong. I couldn't carry the box of books for Susan."

"That's all right. You'll grow, and then your body will be stronger. But God living in you now gives you His kind of strength."

"What kind is that?"

"God's strength is the kind that helps you do what is right. It helps you to love other people, and to want to let God live through you and in you. Remember when Josiah wanted to take your truck with him for his nap? I know you wanted to play with it, but you let him borrow it anyway. Right?"

"Yes. I really didn't want him to have it, but I wanted to be kind."

"Doing good when we don't want to takes God's kind of strength," said Mⓥmmy. "It also pleases God when we use His strength to do His will."

Robby was smiling. "Thank you, Jesus! Now I'm really strong! Just please keep holding me and don't let go."

"He never will," said Mⓥmmy. And He didn't.

M♡mmy,
Will I See Grandma in Heaven?

Linda Hacon Winwood

Anna and Katie sat at the kitchen table coloring their Sunday school lesson about heaven while M♡m prepared dinner. Katie looked up at M♡m and asked, "M♡mmy, will I see Grandma in Heaven?"

"I'm sure you will Katie," M♡m replied. "Why do you ask?"

Katie answered, "Our Sunday school teacher said that only Christians go to heaven and my Grandma isn't a Christian."

"Oh, Katie," M♡m replied, "Grandma's a Christian".

"Oh no, she isn't," Anna added quickly, "Grandma's a Catholic."

M♡m came over to the table and sat down beside the girls. "Anna, Catholics are Christians too."

"But M♡m, if they are Christians, then why do they call themselves Catholics? Does that mean I'm a Catholic too?"

"No Katie," M♡m replied. "Let me see if I can explain it so that you two will understand. You see, girls, the word Catholic means universal and it is also a name of a religious denomination, a special group of Christian believers, like Methodist, Presbyterian, and Baptist. There are many others."

"But, M♡m," asked Anna, "why do they all have different names? Wouldn't it be easier if they all were just called Christians?"

"It sounds like it would be," M♡m agreed, "but people have so many different personalities, customs, and ideas that sometimes it's hard to get everyone to agree on the same things."

"I'm not sure I understand," Katie added, "don't they all follow God's laws and go to church?"

"Yes, Katie, however, I'm afraid it isn't that simple. You see denominations are like clubs. Do you remember last summer when you and Anna started a club and you asked Amy and Brooklyn to join?"

"Yes," Katie replied. "What does that have to do with religions or denominations?"

"I'm getting to that," M♡m answered. "You all had a goal in mind. You set up rules to follow, things you would do, and people you would ask to join your club. You even had a special name picked."

"Yeah," Anna replied, "but it didn't last very long."

"Well, what happened?" asked M♡m.

Katie answered quickly. "Some of the kids didn't like the rules Anna and I started with and they wanted to change the day we were going to meet. Brooklyn wanted to collect dues and Amy didn't have any money, so she quit and then the whole club started to break up. That was when everyone started their own clubs. Now we have four clubs and we all go on picnics and play at the playground at noon. But everyone does things just a little bit different."

"You know girls, that's just what happened to the early believers," replied Mom. "The Bible tells us that God created everything in six days and on the seventh day, He rested. (See Genesis 1&2.) Sunday is the first day of our week; therefore, Saturday was the day of rest for God's people. (See Exodus 31:12-17.) God also told His people to keep that day holy and to worship Him on that day. However, today, because Jesus arose from the dead on a Sunday, most Christian churches have chosen to celebrate Sunday as the day of rest and worship."

"That sounds like a good way to start off the week to me," Anna added.

"I think so too," Mom agreed. "Let's talk about some of the other things we all do, but different. Some churches baptize their members as babies with water sprinkled on their heads, while others baptize when their people are old enough to decide for themselves, like you and Katie did last Sunday." (See Mark 16:16.)

"Yeah," Katie added, "Anna and I went completely under the water just like Jesus did in the Bible."

"Grandma's church worships quietly and some say we make a joyful noise. Many churches fold their hands in prayer, while we lift our hands to pray," added Mom. "We even clap our hands and sometimes Mr. Dan dances in the church just like David did in the Bible."

"Now I'm beginning to understand," Anna replied. "All churches have different names but we're all Christian. Right, Mom?"

"Well, not exactly Anna. Not all religions are Christian religions; only those who follow the teachings of Jesus Christ. Some people are still waiting for the Messiah to come. They don't believe Jesus was the son of God. Some believe He was a prophet just like David, Moses, and Abraham. They believe He is a son of God, just like we are children of God. They don't believe He is God in the flesh or that He rose from the dead. (See John 14, 15, and 16.) We, as Christians, know that He is the son of God and that He has risen from the dead and He is now seated at the right hand of Our Father in Heaven. (See Mark 16:19.) Jesus is also preparing a place for us in heaven right now." (See John 14:2.)

"How can we be sure?" Katie asked.

"The Bible tells us so and we know that the Bible is the Word of God," M♡m answered. It says, in Second Timothy 3:16 (NKJV), 'All scripture is given by inspiration of God, and is profitable for doctrine, for reproof, for correction, for instruction in righteousness.'"

"But, M♡m," Anna asked, "Doesn't everyone believe the Bible?"

"I'm afraid not girls, not everyone follows the teachings of the Bible."

"But, if they don't," asked Katie, "what do they believe?"

"Some groups believe in the Old Testament part of the Bible but not the New. Others say that it is a holy book or a history book, but was for the old days, not for us to follow today. Therefore, many have written their own bibles or religion books. Satan worshipers even have their own bibles."

"Oh, M♡mmy, I bet that makes Jesus very sad," said Katie.

"Yes, it does, girls. The Bible even warns us not to add or take away from the Scriptures. (See Rev. 22:18-19.) God is so loving and patient with us. He is our Heavenly Father. Because He has given us a free will to choose right from wrong, He allows us to do things we shouldn't, knowing we will learn from our mistakes. And, like your Father here on earth, He forgives us when we are truly sorry and turn away from our sins.

"Why don't we get out our Bibles and see what God's Word has to say. It says here, in Exodus chapter 20, that God gave Moses the Ten Commandments. These are God's laws for all His people to follow. If you read them you will see they are still good laws to follow today. But, because we are weak and we all sin, God saw that we needed a Savior—a perfect blood sacrifice to save us from our sins. (See Romans 3:23 and Romans 6:23.) It says in Leviticus 17:11 (NKJV), 'For the life of the flesh is in the blood, and I have given it to you upon the altar to make atonement for your souls; for it is the blood that makes atonement for the soul.'"

"I know," Anna exclaimed, "just like in the Old Testament when people would, once a year, offer up their best lamb or doves to God so that He would forgive their sins." (See Lev. 12:8, 5:11, Luke 2:24.)

"That's right, Anna, it was a symbol of that which was to come, that was Jesus. You see no sacrifice was perfect enough so God sent His only son, Jesus Christ down here to earth to teach us the truth. (See John 3:16.) Jesus was obedient even unto death on the cross as a final payment for our sins. That is why Jesus is called 'The Lamb of God'. (See John 1:29.) Remember in Exodus 12:7-14 when God told the people to put the blood of the lamb on the two doorposts of the house and above the door: 'And when I see the blood, I will pass over you; and the plague shall not be on you to destroy you when I strike the land of Egypt.' And we are to keep it as a feast to the Lord throughout our generations as an everlasting law. This is the feast of the Passover. Jesus was celebrating the 'Passover Supper' the night He was betrayed. (See Matt. 26:26-30, Mark 14:22-26, and Luke 22:14-20.) Jesus took bread and wine and told his disciples that it was His body and blood that would be shed as a forgiveness for our sins and to do it in remembrance of Him. Jesus is the perfect Passover Lamb."

"So it is by the blood of Jesus that we get our salvation," Katie said.

"That's right girls," answered M♡m. "Do you girls remember the story in the Bible when a man named Nicodemus asked Jesus how we can see God and get to Heaven?" (See John 3:3-18.)

"Oh, yes," Anna answered. "Jesus said we must be born again, not of the flesh but in the spirit."

"I know about that," Katie added, "I did that when I confessed that I was a sinner, asked Jesus to forgive my sins, and to come into my heart and be my Savior."

"That's right, girls, and as an outward sign of your commitment to Jesus you decided to get baptized just like Jesus did. When Jesus went to the River Jordan to be baptized, John the Baptist said to Him, 'I ought to be baptized by you and yet you have come to me!' And Jesus replied, 'Let it be so for now, for in this way we shall do all that God requires.' Even Jesus knew He had to be baptized." (See Matthew 3:13-15.)

"That is also when the Holy Spirit came like a dove above Jesus' head and a voice from heaven said, 'This is my beloved Son, in whom I am well pleased,'" Anna added. (See Matt. 3:16-17, Mark 1:9-11, and Luke 3:21-22.)

"Right again! Boy, you girls have really been listening to Pastor Roy's sermons and reading your Bibles. We also believe that when you ask Jesus to live in your heart, that same Holy Spirit comes to live in you, to guide you and give you the strength and power to be more like Jesus. Some Christians believe this happens at baptism." (See John 14 and Romans 8:11-16.)

"M♡mmy, does that mean that all we have to do is confess that we are sinners, believe in Jesus, and we will be saved and go to heaven?" (See Mark 16:16 and Acts 16:31.)

"That's correct, girls. Remember that salvation, or being saved through Jesus, is a free gift from God. There is nothing we can do to earn it. However, to receive a gift we must reach out and take it. (See Rev. 3:20 NKJV) It is a decision we must make for ourselves. No one can make it for us. Jesus said, 'Behold, I stand at the door, and knock; if any man hear my voice, and open the door, I will come in to him, and I will dine with him, and he with me.' Jesus also wants us to obey the

Commandments, follow His example, and share what we know about Him with others. Jesus sets us apart as being His Children. For He has bought us with a price, His Blood."

"I know what else happens when we accept Jesus into our hearts," Katie said. "Our name is written in the Lamb's book of Life. (See Luke 10:20, Daniel 12:1, and Rev. 3-5, 13:8, and 21:27). That's the big book in heaven that tells everyone who can enter. And because my name is written in that book, when I die, I'll get to spend eternal life in heaven with Jesus and Grandma too!"

"Oh, Mommy," Anna said, "it seems so easy. I don't understand why everyone doesn't do it."

"I don't either, Anna. Maybe it's because not everyone knows what God's Word really says because they have never read it for themselves. The Bible says, 'You shall know the truth and it will set you free.' (See John 8:31-32.) Just because you call yourself a Christian and go to church on Sundays doesn't make you a Christian, just like sitting in a garage and making noise like a car doesn't make you a car. In Deuteronomy 6:5, God said we must 'love the Lord our God with all our hearts, with all our soul, and with all our strength.' Jesus tells us to study the scriptures, and go out into the world and tell everyone about Him. (See Matt. 28:18-20 and Mark 16:15.) His message is for all times. You see, girls, the church talked about in the Bible is not any particular building but it is made up of all believers who have accepted Jesus Christ and are truly serving Him. (See Acts 20:28.) All Christian religions might have different rules and ways of doing things, but their ultimate goal is to serve God and get to Heaven through Jesus Christ. God doesn't want us to fight over our differences or be divided by them. Therefore, it doesn't matter what 'club' you or Grandma belong to, but what does matter is that we repent of our sins and are united with God by our faith and love for Jesus. Remember, Jesus said, 'I am the way, the truth and the life, no one comes to the Father but by me.'" (See John 14:6.)

"Do you girls remember the story of Noah's Ark?" M♡m asked.

"Yes," the girls replied.

"But what does that have to do with Jesus?" asked Katie.

"There was only one door into the Ark of safety. Only those who entered through that door were saved. This door is also a type of symbol for Jesus. In John 10:7 Jesus said He is the door. I think some people think the road they follow in life is the only true way to Heaven and everyone else should do it their way. However, I think that when the angel opens that big door or gate to Heaven, my oh my, what a wonderful surprise they will find inside! One big beautiful Heaven filled with people who all believed in Jesus and from all Christian denominations. You maybe surprised at who you will see there. And some may be just as surprised to see you! That is why it's important not to judge a person by what you see. (See Matt. 7:1-5.) Only God has the right to judge. (See Psalm 75:7.) Only He knows what is truly in our hearts." (See 1 Sam. 16:7.)

"Oh, M♡mmy, I can't wait to get to heaven!" said Anna.

"Me, too!" Katie added. "And I want to tell all my friends about Jesus so we can all go to Heaven together."

"Girls, we must go out into the world and tell everyone about Jesus, not just our friends. You see, girls, we are all God's creation, but we are not all children of God. Until we receive Jesus as our Savior that is when we are adopted into the family of God and become His children.

"We are to love and pray even for our enemies. (See Luke 6:27-38.) God has made them and loves them just as much as He does us. It is not God's will for anyone of us to perish. (See Matt. 18:14.) We must let our light shine for all the world to see and follow Jesus." (See Matt. 5-16.)

"I understand now," Anna said.

"Me, too," Katie said as she picked up her paper again. "We better get busy. I want to finish coloring this picture so I can give it to Grandma."

"Me, too," Anna added. "I want her to see just how beautiful it's going to be when we all get to Heaven."

The End…Or is it just the beginning? How about you? Do you have Jesus in your heart? Is your name written in the Lamb's Book of Life?

Behold, I stand at the door and knock. If anyone hears My voice and opens the door, I will come in to him and dine with him and he with Me. (Revelation 3:20 NKJV)

If we confess our sins, He is faithful and just to forgive us our sins and to cleanse us from all unrighteousness. (1 John 1:9 NKJV)

But as many as received Him, to them He gave the right to become children of God, to those who believe in His name. (John 1:12 NKJV)

Holiday
Questions

M♡mmy,
Why Do We Have Easter?

Lou Yohe
Illustrated by Al Berg

"M♡mmy! M♡mmy!" shouted Jimmy as he ran through the house.

"What's the matter Jimmy?" asked M♡mmy.

"Come see what Mrs. Smith is doing to her house!" Jimmy grabbed M♡mmy's hand and pulled her to the front window. "Isn't that neat? Look at all those decorations. I like that big sign that says 'Happy Easter.' Can we decorate our house for Easter too?"

M♡mmy was silent for a moment. Then she asked, "Jimmy, why do we celebrate Easter?"

"Oh, Mommy, you know why we celebrate Easter. We talked about it at Sunday school."

Mommy shook her head. "Jimmy, you didn't answer my question. I asked why do we celebrate Easter?"

"To remember that Jesus died for us," Jimmy replied.

"If we celebrate Easter to remember that Jesus died for us, then why should we decorate our house like Mrs. Smith's?" M♡mmy wanted to know.

"Do I have to answer all these questions?" Jimmy frowned. "Why can't we just decorate our house?"

Jimmy was getting impatient. He pouted a bit as he walked out of the room.

M♡mmy quietly sat down on the sofa, then called her son to her. "Jimmy, please come here."

Jimmy came, but by the look on his face, she knew that he was still pouting.

"Let's talk about this, Jimmy. I didn't say we couldn't decorate our house. But I think it is important that you understand why we celebrate Easter. Perhaps we need to find out why Easter is a holiday. Let's look in the encyclopedia to see what it says about Easter."

Still not feeling cooperative, Jimmy said, "Oh, okay."

He sat still and watched as M♡mmy went to the bookcase and found the volume with an E. Returning to sit beside him, she opened the book. Watching her turn the pages helped Jimmy forget his bad attitude. He started getting excited about what they would find.

"E-A-S-T-E-R," spelled M♡mmy. "Here it is. Listen while I read to you."

"Easter is a Christian festival that celebrates the resurrection of Jesus Christ. It is the most important holy day of the Christian religion."

M♡mmy paused. "Jimmy, do you know what resurrection means?"

"I think…it means that when Jesus died, He came alive again three days later," Jimmy responded. "Wait a minute," he said as he looked up at his M♡mmy with big eyes. "If Easter is for celebrating Jesus' resurrection, then why didn't Mrs. Smith have anything about Jesus around her house? She just had lambs, rabbits, and Easter eggs."

"That's a good question. Let's read some more in the encyclopedia," M♡mmy answered.

"One legend says that a poor woman dyed some eggs during a famine, and hid them in a nest as an Easter gift for her children. Just as the children discovered the nest, a big rabbit leaped away. The story spread that the rabbit had brought the Easter eggs."

"M♡mmy, I'll be right back," interrupted Jimmy. He jumped off the sofa and ran out of the living room.

In a flash he returned with his Bible storybook. Quickly he flipped through the pages to the pictures of Jesus hanging on the cross.

He stopped and gazed at the picture. He didn't say anything. M♡mmy sat and watched him for a few minutes. Finally she said, "What are you thinking, Jimmy?"

Jimmy didn't reply immediately, but M♡mmy waited patiently. Then he said, "M♡mmy, I want to let everyone know why we celebrate Easter. What Jesus did for us makes Easter the best day of the year. Boy, do people have the wrong reason for celebrating Easter."

"What do you mean?" questioned M♡mmy.

"Well, Jesus had to die because of all the bad things I do. My Sunday school teacher calls it sin," said Jimmy thoughtfully as he turned back pages to the beginning of the Bible storybook.

He pointed to a picture of Adam and Eve in the Garden of Eden. "First Adam and Eve were happy—then they disobeyed God. That's when sin came." He turned to the next page, which showed the ark with lots of animals around it. "God told Noah to build an ark and the big flood came. But that didn't help because people just wouldn't listen to God. So God sent Jesus."

Continuing to page through the Bible storybook, he stopped at the picture of Baby Jesus in a manger. "Christmas is Jesus' birthday," Jimmy said.

Jimmy grinned up at his M♡mmy. "Gee, M♡mmy, I can't believe how much fun I'm having doing all this…what does Daddy call it when he needs to know something?"

"Research," replied M♡mmy.

"We're doing research just like Daddy," laughed Jimmy.

"I'm amazed how much you have learned about Jesus," said M♡mmy, as she gave Jimmy a big hug. "Shall we do some more 'research'?"

Mommy picked up her Bible and said, "Jesus was 33 years old when He was baptized and began His ministry. 'Behold, the Lamb of God who takes away the sin of the world!' John the Baptist spoke those words when he baptized Jesus."

"Is that why the lamb is important to Easter? Mrs. Smith put one on her lawn," said Jimmy.

Mommy nodded and continued. "Jesus went from place to place telling everyone that he was the Son of God. Then one day Jesus told His disciples that He would soon die. While in Jerusalem, the soldiers came and they hung Jesus on the cross. His friends were very sad when he died. But his friends took his body and put it in a tomb."

"I remember," said Jimmy. "And the next day was like our Sunday."

"That's right," Mommy agreed. She opened her Bible again and began to read, "'Now on the first day of the week Mary Magdalene came early to the tomb, while it was still dark, and saw the stone already taken away from the tomb.' When Mary went into the tomb she saw an angel in a white robe. He said, 'You are looking for Jesus who has been crucified. He is not here, for He has risen.'" (See Matthew 28:2-6.)

"Wow! That must have been exciting!" Jimmy exclaimed. "And that happened on the first day of the week. Sunday is our first day of the week, so I guess that's why every Sunday we celebrate that Jesus is in heaven, getting ready for us to join him."

"Jimmy," Mommy continued, "I have a suggestion. Since Easter is the most important day for Christians, even more important than Christmas, let's have a Resurrection Party on Easter Sunday. You know Daddy likes to have a party on 'Super Bowl Sunday,' especially if he thinks his team is going to win. We would celebrate the victory over sin Jesus won for us when he died on the cross and rose again from the dead. What do you think?"

"That's a neat idea," Jimmy shouted as he jumped up and down in excitement.

"So you don't want to decorate the house for Easter?" asked Mommy.

After thinking for a minute, Jimmy looked up at his Mommy and said, "Maybe we could make a cross and put it in our yard with a lamb beside it. Daddy could make a sign that says: JESUS WINS! But the party is the best idea. In fact, let's invite Mrs. Smith so she can learn the real reason we celebrate Easter!" Jimmy declared.

Mommy nodded and smiled as Jimmy kept thinking of plans for their Resurrection Party. This year Easter would be a very special day.

M♡mmy,
Is There an Easter Bunny?

Barbara Knoll
Illustrated by Al Berg

"M♡mmy," said Julie, dropping her jacket on the floor as she walked into the house, "Tom from next door was talking about the Easter Bunny. He was telling me about all the presents and candy he gets for Easter."

"That's nice, honey," said M♡mmy without looking up. She was working, typing at the computer. "Please put your jacket away, dear."

"M♡mmy," said Julie as she hung up her jacket, "I know that Easter isn't just about bunnies and presents. But is there an Easter Bunny? A real one?"

M♡mmy turned to her and smiled. "Julie, we've already talked about this, remember? I'm a little busy right now. Why don't you get out your Easter book? You can choose a story for me to read to you when I've finished this job."

Julie smiled and nodded, and M♡mmy turned back to the computer.

Julie went over to the bookcase. She pulled out some books without finding the Easter book. Oh! There it was, on the top shelf. Standing on the books she'd already taken out, she just managed to grab the one she wanted before she slid to the floor. Sitting among the other books, she began to look through it.

The book opened at the picture of Jesus on the cross. Julie looked at it sadly before turning the page. There was the empty tomb with the stone rolled away—much better! Julie didn't like to think of those people killing Jesus. After all, He was God's own Son! He had never done anything wrong. And He loved her, and everyone else, too. Nobody should be mean to Jesus!

Julie stopped at a page that showed a lovely green meadow surrounded by a forest. There were wildflowers everywhere. Here and there were a few large rocks, and some holes in the ground. Also on this page were rabbits. There were big rabbits and little rabbits; some were white and some brown. Staring at the picture, Julie decided she liked the brown rabbits better. They seemed friendlier somehow, and softer.

As she looked at the page and thought about the rabbits, she wandered into her imagination. All of a sudden Julie felt herself growing smaller and smaller, until she could fit onto the page. Still she shrank, until she was just the size of the rabbits. Then, taking a deep breath, she jumped…

Julie just missed landing in one of the holes. A brown rabbit poked his head out of it.

"What do you think you're doing?" he asked, jumping out of the hole. "This is my hole, and you'll come in when I invite you!"

"I'm sorry," said Julie. "I guess I didn't aim my jump very well."

"I guess not," said the rabbit. He was still a little cross. His ears drooped as he patted at the dirt around his hole. Then he turned to look at Julie. "What are you doing here?" he asked. "We don't get many of your kind. In fact, I think you're the first one."

"Oh," said Julie. "I've been wondering about the Easter Bunny. Does he live around here?" she asked hopefully.

The rabbit's ears pointed straight up again. "Yes, he does," the rabbit said proudly. "You're inside the Easter book, and you're talking to the Easter Bunny."

"You're the Easter Bunny?" asked Julie. She hadn't realized she'd find him on her first try.

"Well," he said modestly, "I'm one of them."

"Do you mean there are more than one?" asked Julie.

"We rabbits aren't known for living alone," he answered. "What exactly did you want to know?"

"I guess I wanted to know how you started," Julie said.

The rabbit winked at her. "Do you want to know how rabbits got started, or why people think we bring eggs and jelly beans, or about the Easter Bunny?"

Julie was confused. "All of them, I guess."

"Follow me, then," said the rabbit, hopping down into his hole. It seemed to Julie that they traveled very far down, then across, then up. The hole was dark, but it smelled like good, clean mud. The rabbit was still talking. "Where we rabbits got started was in the beginning. God made us. He did a good job, too, didn't He?"

"A very good job," Julie answered, hiding a smile. "What about bringing eggs and things? When did that start?"

"I'll show you, if you'll just hop up here," said the rabbit. They both jumped out of the hole.

Julie looked around. She saw a boy and a girl who seemed excited as they discovered a nest full of colored eggs behind a rock. The boy was holding an egg and pointing at a bunny which was hopping away. A lady was peeking out from behind a tree and smiling.

"Where are we?" Julie asked.

"Page 32," said the rabbit. "'The Legend of the Easter Bunny'."

"Oh," said Julie. "What's going on?"

"Well, this is how the story of the Easter Bunny probably started. You see that lady? That's the children's Mother. A long time ago, a Mother colored some eggs and put them in a small nest outside for her children to find at Easter. Just as they found the eggs, a large rabbit hopped away. The children thought he had left the eggs, and the story spread from there."

"That makes sense," said Julie. "That's how it is at our house. Mommy and Daddy give me treats at Easter because they love me, and to help celebrate."

"Did you want to hear about the Easter Bunny?" asked the rabbit.

"I thought I just did," said Julie, confused.

"You heard the part about the presents and eggs and candy," the rabbit answered. "But we rabbits like to think there's more to it than that. At Easter time, you see us everywhere—on pictures and in cartoons, and even made of chocolate. Well, there's more to us than eggs and jelly beans! Follow me!"

Once again, Julie found herself following the rabbit along a dark tunnel. They came up out of the hole at a place Julie already knew. But she'd never been so close before. Looking up, Julie began to cry. The rabbit passed her a white handkerchief.

"This is a sad page, isn't it?" he said. "This is where Jesus is giving His life for all the world. But if He hadn't done that, then He would never have been able to have you live with Him."

"And He wouldn't be able to live in my heart, either," sniffled Julie.

"We're going somewhere else now," said the rabbit. "Think about what happened to Jesus after He died." With that, he popped back down the hole. Julie didn't have any choice except to follow him.

The rabbit paused just before they went up into the light. "After Jesus died on the cross, where did they put His body?" he asked.

"In a cave-tomb," answered Julie.

"And where do rabbits and bunnies live?"

"In burrows under the ground," answered Julie. "Oh! I see! Rabbits stay under the ground like Jesus did. And when you come out of your hole, it's kind of like how Jesus came out of the tomb!"

"That's how we rabbits like to think of it. We're not just bringers of gifts, but reminders of the resurrection—of Jesus being alive again!" With a wink, the rabbit jumped out of the hole. Julie jumped too…and landed on page 9—her favorite page! She ran to look inside Jesus' cave-tomb.

It really was empty! There were the cloths they had wrapped Jesus' body in, just as in her Bible story! She turned to talk to the rabbit…

"Julie!" called a familiar voice, startling her. Julie felt herself growing and growing, getting bigger and bigger. "Good-bye!" she called softly to the rabbit. "Thank you!"

Mﾟmmy walked into the room. "Thank you for waiting, honey," she said, leaning down to hug Julie. "I'm finally finished with that job. Did you decide which story you want me to read to you?"

Julie showed her Mﾟther the page with the bunnies on it. Mﾟmmy read to her about rabbits and eggs and springtime. When they were finished, Julie said, "Thanks, Mﾟmmy. Can we read another story later?"

"Sure, honey," said Mﾟmmy. "But I'd like you to do me a favor. Please pick up these books you dropped. Sometimes I think you're the droppingest person I know. I'm glad you're also one of the picking-uppest ones!"

As Mﾟmmy left the room, Julie began to clean up the books. She smiled to herself. Mﾟmmy was right. She did seem to drop things a lot; there was just too much to think about. Like that nice rabbit…

Suddenly Julie dropped the book she was putting away. She grabbed the Easter book and turned to page 9. There was the empty tomb with the stone rolled away. She looked more closely. Oh dear! She'd done it again!

Down at the corner, beside a rabbit-sized hole, lay a tiny white handkerchief. Julie was sure she hadn't seen it there before. The brown rabbit beside the hole turned his head toward her a little. He winked.

M♡mmy,
Why Don't We Celebrate Halloween?

Linda Hacon Winwood
Illustrated by Al Berg

"**O**ctober 31 again and all the kids are trick-or-treating," said Jerry as he looked out the window in front of his house. "M♡m, why can't we go trick-or-treating like all the other kids? Are you afraid we'll eat too much candy and our teeth will rot?"

"Well, Jerry," said M♡m, I certainly don't want your teeth to rot, but no, that isn't the reason you can't go trick-or-treating. As Christians, Daddy and I don't let you take part in Halloween because we know Jesus doesn't want us to do such things."

"But why, M♡mmy?" Sarah exclaimed. "What's wrong with Halloween?"

"Think for a moment, children, about other holidays we celebrate. Take Christmas, for example. How does Christmas make you feel?" asked M♡m.

"Happy!" exclaimed Sarah.

"Excited," added Jerry.

"That's right," said M♡m. "Christmas is a time of happiness and excitement as we celebrate the birth of Baby Jesus. Do you remember what the angel told the shepherds the night He was born?"

"Yes," said Sarah. "The angel told the shepherds good news of peace and great joy."

"That's right," said M♡m. "Halloween has none of these. Halloween is filled with fear, meanness, and sadness."

"I don't understand, M♡m," said Jerry. "How is dressing up in funny costumes and going door-to-door to get candy, scary and sad?"

"The devil is very good at making things look wonderful on the outside that are wrong on the inside. Halloween is one of those things," Mom said.

"Many Christians haven't been taught the true meaning behind Halloween. They can't see the truth behind the costumes, parades, and candy of Halloween," continued Mom. "Only when we know the truth about something can we know whether it is good or bad for us. That's why the Bible says in John 8:32 that we are free when we know the truth."

"So, what's the truth about Halloween, M♡m?" Sarah asked. "Why shouldn't Christians take part in its fun?"

"Let me see if I can explain it a bit better," M♡m said. "First, let's think about Christmas again. When the three wise men came to visit Baby Jesus, what did they bring Him."

"Presents!" Sarah said.

"Yes, presents," Mℴm agreed. "When they gave Jesus the presents, the wise men knelt before Jesus to show that they honored Him."

"What does it mean to honor someone?" Jerry asked.

"To honor someone means that you show great respect for that person. You show that you understand his importance and great worth," Mℴm replied.

"But we don't kneel before anyone at Halloween," Sarah protested.

"You see, Sarah," Mℴm said, "there are many ways to show honor. One way is to set aside a special day, a holiday, to remember some important person or event."

"Yes!" Jerry agreed. "Thanksgiving reminds us of the big dinner the Pilgrims shared with the Indians to thank God for His help in the New World."

"Exactly," Mom responded. "What event do we celebrate at Easter?"

"That's when the angel rolled away the stone," Sarah answered. "Jesus wasn't dead anymore!"

"That's right," Mom replied. "At Easter we remember God's love when He sent Jesus to die on the Cross for our sins. We also honor God for His great power that brought Jesus from death to life."

"So what do we honor at Halloween?" Jerry asked.

"A long time ago," Mom answered, "many people did not believe in God or honor His Son, Jesus. Instead they honored statues made of wood or stone. They also worshiped things in nature like the sun and the stars."

"Do you mean they bowed down to them like the wise men knelt before Baby Jesus?" Sarah asked.

"Yes, Sarah," Mom said. "They sang praises to their statues just like we sing praises to Jesus. They believed that the sun and stars had great power."

"God must not have liked that! He wants us to worship only Him," Jerry said.

"You are right, Jerry," Mom replied. "God's first laws for His people teach us not to worship any other gods or to bow down to their statues." (See Exodus 20:3-5.)

"But, Mommy, we don't worship any statues or other gods at Halloween," Sarah said.

"In many parts of the world," Mom answered, "Halloween is a religious holiday—a holiday when people worship satan and honor evil. In fact, it is the biggest holiday on satan's calendar, kind of like Christmas and Easter on our calendar."

"But why?" Jerry asked. "Where's the evil in Halloween?"

"Long ago the people who worshiped statues and nature also believed that the spirits of the dead could control the living," M♡m said. "They thought that the souls of wicked people who had died returned on Halloween to harm or scare the living."

"That sounds dumb," said Jerry.

"These people didn't think so," M♡m replied. "So they tried to keep the evil spirits happy by setting out sweets and other types of treats. They wanted the evil spirits to stay away and not trick them."

"Oh, I see," said Sarah, "and that's also where the trick-or-treat part of Halloween comes from."

"That's right," said Mom. "A group of farmers in Ireland, called Celts, asked everyone in the village to bring food to a town party. Then they gave the food to the evil spirits by burning it in a big bonfire. They even burned animals to feed the spirits. Many villagers wore costumes to the bonfire."

M♡m continued. "They were made of animal skins and bones. Some farmers also wore animal heads. This is how the tradition of dressing up got started."

"What about the pumpkins, M♡m? How did they become part of Halloween?" Jerry asked.

"The pumpkin part of Halloween started from the story of a man named Jack," Mom said. "People believed that after he died he walked around the earth carrying a lantern.

"So folks would hollow out pumpkins or turnips and put candles in them. Then they set the pumpkins and turnips outside their front gates to scare away the evil spirits who might think Jack was there. That's why they are called Jack-o-lanterns," Mom said.

"That makes sense," Sarah replied.

"Do you see," Mom asked, "how Halloween centers around evil, scary things? In fact, many costumes picture witches, ghosts, goblins, and other evil creatures that are enemies of God.

"Jesus does not want us to have anything to do with evil," M♡m added. "It says that in Deuteronomy 18:13-14. If we are Jesus' friends, how can we have fun when we look and act like His enemies? Joy comes from being like Jesus."

"If Halloween is so evil, why do so many Christian schools and churches still go trick-or-treating, march in parades, and have Halloween parties?" Jerry asked.

"Hundreds of years ago," M♡m said, "the rulers of Rome passed a law that everyone had to accept Christianity, the new state religion. Most people became Christians because they had to, not because they wanted to. Instead of giving up their wicked beliefs and the worship of other gods, they added these things to Christianity. Halloween is one example of this.

"When the rulers of Rome tried to stop Halloween parties, the people became angry. They saw nothing wrong with mixing their false beliefs with the worship of Jesus.

"So the Roman rulers moved a Christian holiday, All Saints Day, to November 1 and gave October 31 the name Halloween, which means Holy Evening. Then they told the people to pray for the dead on Halloween, instead of praying to other gods."

"So Halloween became a religious holiday because the Roman leaders changed its name?" Jerry asked.

"Not really," Mom said. "Halloween was always a religious holiday, but it wasn't a Christian holiday. It still isn't.

"Changing the name of something doesn't change what it is," Mom added. "If I call you Sarah instead of Jerry, that doesn't make you Sarah. It only changes what I call you. So the name, Halloween, doesn't change what is really happening on October 31. It's just playing 'Let's Make a Deal' with the devil."

"I wouldn't want to do that," Jerry said.

"Me neither," Sarah added.

"So is Halloween still a holy evening?" Jerry asked.

"Not for Christians," Mom answered. "The activities of Halloween lead us to believe that satan and his followers have power over our lives. This is not true. The Bible tells us in First John 4:4 that Jesus is greater and more powerful than any evil spirit. Nothing can harm us when we are under His protection."

"Mommy, do you really believe all these things?" Sarah asked.

"Yes I do, Sarah," Mom replied. "Some people think I'm making a big deal over nothing, but God has placed Daddy and me over you to protect you and to teach you about Jesus. The Bible tells us that in Proverbs 22:6. We are not willing to give satan the tiniest crack to enter your lives and hurt you. It's the joy, peace, and good news of Jesus that we want to plant in your hearts and minds. We cannot allow you to do something we know dishonors Him. That's why we don't permit Halloween in our home.

"The Bible teaches us in Colossians 3:17 to do and say everything in the name of Jesus," M♡m added. "We certainly can't take part in Halloween in His name. Yet there are many things we can enjoy because Jesus is a Friend who shares love and joy. He wants us to have fun doing good things that bring us laughter, friendship, and peace."

"I think I understand a little better now, M♡m," Jerry said. "You want us to honor and obey Jesus, not satan."

"That's right, Jerry," Mom answered. "As Christians, we shouldn't allow anything that even looks like evil to be part of our lives. We read that in First Thessalonians 5:22."

"It's not easy to honor Jesus when we can't share in the fun other kids have," Sarah said.

"Remember, children," Mom warned, "what you choose to do for fun must never harm your relationship with Jesus. You cannot grow in your friendship with Him if you do things that dishonor Him.

"Instead of following the example of your friends as they dress up and go trick-or-treating, you need to think of other fun things to do on Halloween night," Mom suggested. "Maybe you two would like to fold socks and do the dishes tonight."

"Come on, Mom! Since when are chores fun?!" asked Jerry.

Mom chuckled and put her arms around Sarah and Jerry. "Think of all the work the children in the Bible did!"

"Yeah!" Sarah agreed as she grinned. "Just think, Jerry, you can do chores for seven years plus another seven years for the privilege of marrying your true love, like Jacob worked for Rachel. I read that in Genesis chapter 29."

"Oh yeah?" Jerry objected. "That certainly doesn't sound like fun to me."

"Seriously, children," M♡m said, "your Dad and I have planned a special family time for this evening. We thought we'd all go out for pizza and a movie."

"That's a great idea, M♡m!" Sarah agreed.

Jerry gave his M♡m a big hug and said, "I love you, M♡m. The next time someone asks me why we don't celebrate Halloween, I know just what to say."

Daddy,
Are You Santa Claus?

Galen Burkholder
Illustrated by Al Berg

"Good morning children," Daddy said as he came to the top of the stair steps. "I know it is Saturday, but rise and shine," he added. "Mommy and I have been up for several hours and already the Christmas tree has been set up in the corner of the living room. We need to decorate it today, and everyone must do their part; Christmas is only a couple of weeks away."

After eating the breakfast that Mommy had made, everyone gathered in the living room for the annual Christmas tree decorating.

Daddy was right; there was something for everyone to do. First the lights had to be stretched out and plugged into the wall to make sure that each bulb would light up. Then Matthew and David held the long strands of lights so Daddy could place them on the tree.

As Daddy made the first complete wrap of lights around the tree Matthew asked, "Daddy, are you Santa Claus?" "Yeah, are you Daddy?" Trisha added. M♡mmy had a big smile as she waited to see what Daddy would say.

"Do you think I am?" was Daddy's reply. Matthew said "no;" David said "I don't know;" and "yes" was Trisha's answer.

"Trisha, you said you thought I was Santa Claus. How do you know there is a Santa Claus?" As her older brothers looked at each other Trisha answered, "Because he brings us presents. And they are always what we want," she added. "If you're not Santa, then how does Santa Claus know what to bring us?"

Daddy paused for a moment then said, "Don't you remember that each year around Thanksgiving time you write a letter to Santa and put it in the mailbox? Then a week or so later when we went shopping you sat on his lap and told him your wish list so he could choose several things from it to bring to you. Now I was with you when you spoke to him. How could I be Santa Claus?"

"But Daddy," David added, "we went to several stores and when we were there we saw Santa Claus." Matthew shook his head yes and agreed.

"So I guess you are asking me if there is more than one Santa Claus or how did he get to the other stores before us? Do you believe there is more than one Santa Claus?" Daddy asked. "Yes," "maybe," and "I don't know" were the children's replies.

"Let's pretend that there is more than one Santa Claus. Then I suppose that there could be a different Santa Claus for different children. Does that really make any difference as long as you get a gift from him?" Daddy asked. The children agreed on this question and the answer was "no!"

"OK, it's time to put the bulbs and decorations on the tree," Daddy announced. Trisha held the boxes so M♡mmy could place the bulbs and other ornaments on the tree.

As Daddy stepped back to make room for M♡mmy and Trisha he asked, "Do you think Santa Claus only gives gifts to those who get him a gift?"

"Well, we put out cookies and milk, but probably not everyone does that," David replied.

"Then we could say that it is more important to Santa Claus to give gifts than to receive gifts," Daddy said. "That sounds familiar, doesn't it?" he added. "That sounds like what M♡mmy and Daddy and your Sunday school teacher have taught you, that 'it is more blessed to give than to receive.'"

Daddy continued saying, "That reminds us that Christmas is actually a birthday, the birthday of Jesus, God's Son. On Christmas day, God gave His greatest gift, Jesus, who He sent into the world so each of us can live with him after our bodies die. Jesus gives us gifts and blessings every day of our lives."

"Daddy," Matthew said, "If we have Jesus and he gives us gifts, why do we need Santa Claus?"

"That's a very good question," Daddy said. "Not everyone believes in Jesus," he added and then paused. "That looks very nice," he told Trisha and M♡mmy as they finished their decorating.

As Daddy began to hang tinsel on the tree he asked, "Is there any reason why we can't believe in both? After all, both Santa and Jesus have taught us that there is joy in giving."

Daddy stepped back away from the tree and then with a look of happiness on his face he said, "OK, someone hand me the angel for on top of the tree and we'll be all ready for Christmas and Santa Claus."

"But Daddy, are you Santa Claus? Are you our Santa Claus?" Trisha asked.

"Well, children, you've finally got me. I am indeed your Santa Claus. Just as our heavenly Father enjoys giving us gifts and blessings, so I enjoy giving gifts to you, my children." With a wink toward M♡mmy, Daddy said, "And you can give a gift too by remembering the milk and cookies again this year.

"Now everyone into the car and let's go get some burgers and fries."

M♡mmy,
Was Santa Claus Born on Christmas, Too?

Barbara Knoll
Illustrated by Al Berg

"Won't Dad be surprised when he comes home? The tree will look so beautiful!"

"Here, honey," said Rachel's M♡m, "I think you're big enough this year to hang these up yourself."

"Ooh!" Rachel breathed. "These are my favorites!" Carefully opening the box, she took out the special Nativity ornaments one by one. "Here's Mary, Jesus' M♡ther. And this is Joseph, who was an earthly Daddy for Him. And the angels—I'll hang them higher so they look like they're flying and singing. Here come the shepherds and the little woolly lambs…" As she slowly spoke, Rachel hung each ornament on the tree. The ornament of the Baby was placed gently in a cradle on a nearby table; He would be added to the tree on Christmas Day. For now they would await Jesus' birth together.

Then Rachel noticed something else in the box. What was that flash of red? Puzzled, she pulled out another ornament. This one was a round, jolly fellow carrying a huge bag on his back. What was Santa doing with the Nativity ornaments?

"M♡m, I understand that at Christmas we celebrate Jesus' birth. We celebrate His life, and how He came to show us what God is like. I know about the angels and the shepherds and the wise men…but what about Santa? How does he fit in? Was Santa Claus born on Christmas, too?"

M♡m smiled. "Don't you remember, sweetie? We've talked about that. You go find your Christmas book, and we'll talk about it again. But I've got to go check on those cookies we put in the oven."

Rachel went over to the bookcase. Pulling out her favorite Christmas book, she sat down, holding the Santa ornament, to look at it.

The book fell open to a picture of a ship in a storm. Most of the sailors looked terrified! But one man was on his knees, praying. Why was he doing that? Why wasn't he helping the men try to control the boat?

Thinking about the picture and the man who was praying, Rachel looked again at the ornament. The smile on Santa's face seemed to grow wiser. He almost seemed to wink at her. Smiling absently down at Santa, Rachel wandered into her imagination. She felt herself growing smaller, until she could fit onto the page. Something wet was lashing her cheeks, and her hair was blowing wildly in the wind. Ignored by most of the men, she crept quietly forward toward the one who was praying.

Sensing her approach, he turned and smiled at her. Suddenly she realized the storm had stopped. The man's prayer had been answered!

"Are you…Jesus?" she asked, barely able to speak. She knew that Jesus had calmed a storm once.

"No," he replied with a smile. "I am Nicholas, a follower of Jesus. I was on my way home from visiting the land of Israel when this storm came up. But the Lord has heard my prayer and calmed the storm. Tomorrow I will go to the church at Myra to thank Him for saving us all."

As the men came up to speak with Nicholas and exclaim over the sudden calm, Rachel remembered something. The next day, he would go to that church. He didn't know it, but their elderly bishop had died. The Lord had told the eldest bishop that the first person to enter the church the next morning would be the new bishop. And that person would be Nicholas!

Still daydreaming, Rachel turned to another page in the book.

She remembered this picture well. It showed a tall, thin man dressed in a hooded cloak. He held a small bag in one hand and was walking with his head down, so that his face was in the shadow. Rachel was fascinated by this picture. The man looked so mysterious!

Hurrying, she tried to catch up to Nicholas. Suddenly he stopped just outside a house. With a quick movement, he tossed something in through the window! Rachel cringed, waiting for the sound of shattering glass. Then she remembered: there was no glass in the windows here.

A man ran out of the house. Would he yell at Nicholas for throwing things at his home? As Rachel watched, the man embraced Nicholas, thanking him over and over. Seeing Rachel, he exclaimed, "What do you think this man has done? I have three daughters. Daughters I am rich with, money I am not. Each time my daughters have come to the age of marrying, the money for the dowry, the gift for the groom, has appeared in my home. This time, for my third daughter, I waited. I knew I could catch our generous friend. And see? It is none other than the big-hearted Nicholas! He has saved my daughters from being sold as servants!"

"Shh! Please, my friend. Don't tell anyone what I have done—at least until after I've died. I want to honor God by giving in secret, as Christ Jesus taught us to do."

"Don't tell anyone? Not even about your remarkable aim? Look!" As the man pointed, laughing, Rachel knew what she would see. The bag of coins had landed in a newly washed stocking, hung by the chimney to dry.

She smiled at the Santa ornament. "That's why we hang our stockings by the chimney for you to fill."

Rachel's M♡m came into the room carrying a plate of cookies and a glass of milk. With a smile she laid them on a table near Rachel. "It sounds like you're remembering the story after all," she said.

Rachel looked at the picture in the book again. Then she looked at the ornament. "How did Saint Nicholas change to Santa Claus?"

"It took a lot of time and several nations," answered her M♡m. "When people moved from place to place, they took the idea of Saint Nicholas with them. Over time, people changed parts of the story. They even changed his personality and what he stood for. Instead of a devoted man of God known for his generosity to the poor, he became a jolly old gift-giver.

"You see, the Santa you know about is based on a real man, almost as if Saint Nicholas is Santa's great-grandfather from long ago. Stories of Santa are found in some form throughout the world, wherever people celebrate Christ's birth. That's because people all over the world tell stories about the giving and generous stranger who loves children and who brings gifts to them at Christmas."

"That's kind of like what God did," Rachel mused. "At Christmas, God gave us the gift of Jesus."

"That's right, Rachel," answered M♡m. "At the time Jesus came to the earth, most people didn't really know God. So He was almost a stranger to them. But God's gift had a special purpose: He gave us His Son so we could know Him!"

Smiling, Rachel hung the Santa ornament on the tree. As she glanced at it, she gasped.

Did he just wink at her?

Daddy,
Does God Take a Vacation?

Galen C. Burkholder
Illustrated by Al Berg

"Good morning Bethany, good morning Timothy," Daddy said as they came to the breakfast table rubbing their eyes in disbelief that it was morning already.

"You guys really need to eat a good breakfast today," Mommy said. "We still have a lot to do before we leave for vacation." Then Daddy said the blessing on the meal.

"Daddy, can we go back to bed again after we eat?" Timmy asked. "We're still tired from all the packing and extra work we did yesterday getting ready for our trip."

Bethany shook her head yes. "Yes Daddy, why can't we sleep late on the second day of our vacation just like the first?"

"Well," Daddy said, "remember how we chose where we wanted to go during our vacation? Extra sleep is OK, but we are taking a vacation so we can spend extra time together as a family."

"Daddy, does God ever get tired?" Timmy asked.

"Yeah, does He ever sleep?" Bethany added.

"Whoa, kids, one question at a time. Those are good questions. In God's Word he tells us that in six days he created the world and on the seventh day he rested. It says He rested, it doesn't say He was tired. His Word also tells us that he knows every thing we think, do, and say. If He can do that, certainly God never sleeps. He can do that because He is God.

"But we are his people and we get tired and we need to sleep. God knows that we need to rest from what we do at least one day a week. When we take a vacation, that is extra time that we can get away from the things we normally do every day."

"Doesn't taking a vacation cost a lot of money?" Bethany asked.

"Yeah, where does the money come from?" Timmy added.

"We have money for this vacation because we saved money for it. God has blessed Daddy and Mommy with good jobs so that we can provide for the needs of our family," Daddy said.

"Why else do we take a vacation?" Timmy asked.

"We take a vacation so we can play and have fun together. It's a time when we can travel and see this big beautiful world God has created. It's a time when we can make new friends and meet new people. It's a time for your M♡ther and I to get a break from our jobs.

"Speaking of breaks," Daddy continued, "I need a break from all these questions. Now that you have finished your breakfast, it's time you two get out of your PJs and get dressed. Make sure you have your favorite books, games, and stuffed animals to keep you busy while we travel in the car."

Timmy went to his room. He knew that he had packed his swimsuit, but he wanted to take his ball glove, his favorite game, and of course his stuffed puppy. He also wanted to take a pencil and some paper; that would help make the trip go faster. He put all these things into a blue tote bag.

Bethany went to her room. She knew that she had packed her swimsuit, but she wanted to take her favorite game and her favorite doll. She checked to make sure that she had enough clothes for her doll so that she would have clothes to play in, clothes to eat in, and dressy clothes to wear each evening. Bethany knew that making plans for her doll would keep her busy during much of the trip. And of course she had to make sure to take her doll's hair brush. She put all her final choices into a pink tote bag.

Now that Timmy and Bethany had made their final choices, with their tote bags in their hands they each took a final glance into their rooms and then hurried off to the car. They wanted to please M♡mmy and Daddy and they didn't want to keep them waiting.

214

When they got to the car M♡mmy was bringing out the last of the suitcases. Daddy had checked the car to make sure that it was ready for the trip. He had checked under the hood, checked the tires, checked all the lights and turning signals, and had put almost everything into the car's trunk.

"Daddy, does God ever take a break from us?" Bethany asked.

"Yeah, does God ever take a vacation?" Timmy added.

"Hmm. Since we've been working real hard to get everything finished," Daddy said, "how about we take a break for a minute. Let's all sit down on the grass in the shade and talk about it."

After everyone sat down under a big shade tree, Daddy asked, "Do you guys remember the story about David and Goliath?"

"Yeah, I do," Timmy said. "He was the little boy who whopped up on the big giant who was an enemy. And he killed him with just a little stone."

"Do you remember the story about Moses and how he held his hands up and parted the Red Sea so all his people could escape the enemy?" Daddy asked. They both shook their heads yes. "Who remembers the story about Jonah?"

"I do," Bethany answered. "He was the guy that tried to run away from God and the big fish got him. Then he changed his mind."

"That's right," Daddy said. "In each case God helped his servants when they needed Him. If God would have been taking a break, how would he have known that they needed Him?

"God's Word tells us that He will never leave us alone. It tells us that He will go with us, He will fight our enemies, He will save us and keep us safe. It tells us that He will go with us even until the end of the world. That's why when Mommy and I prayed this morning we prayed that He would keep us safe as we travel. We know that He can do that because God is so big that He gives each of us all of His time.

"I can see by looking at your faces you want to know how I know that. In God's Word we read that even a little bird does not get hurt without God knowing it. God tells us that even the hairs on our head are numbered; we are much more important to God than the birds," Daddy said.

"Can you see why a God that powerful and all-knowing doesn't need to take a vacation? But if you keep asking all these good questions, we will never get our own vacation," Daddy said with a laugh. "Hold all your other questions until we get back. Race you to the car." Daddy, Bethany, and Timmy all ran laughing to the car.

Bonus
Stories

Colored Eggs for Jesse

Linda Hacon Winwood
Illustrated by Tony Casino

Jesse ran into the kitchen and gave his grandma a great big hug.

"Hi, Jesse," Grandma said. "I'm so glad you came to see me today. I have a special surprise for you." Grandma handed Jesse a bright colored package.

"A present for me? What's in it Grandma?"

Before opening it, Jesse gave it a squeeze. Then he ripped off the colored paper and revealed a carton of bright colored plastic eggs.

Mommy smiled and said to Grandma, "Oh, Mom, I can't believe you saved them after all these years! Jesse, when I was your age, Grandma gave the same present to me."

"What's in them Grandma? Candy?"

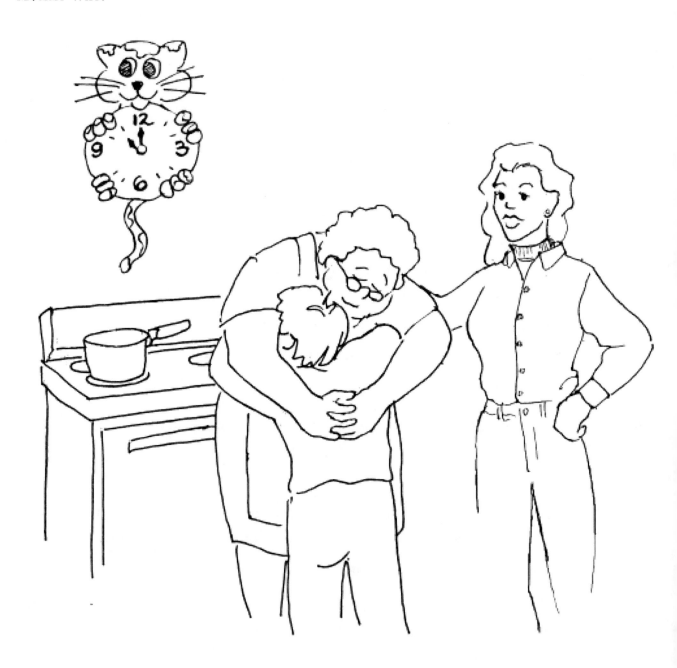

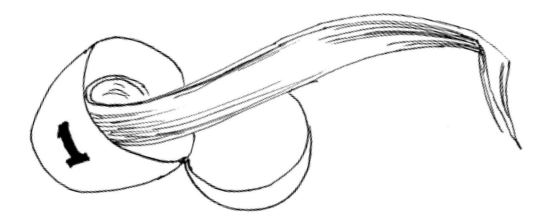

"Well, why don't you open them and see?" replied M♡m.

"Before we do," Grandma added, "I want you to know that these are not just ordinary colored eggs. These are the same eggs I gave your M♡mmy when she was my little girl. And that what is inside will help to remind us all of the real Easter Story."

"You mean the story about Jesus, don't you Grandma?" Jesse answered.

"That's right," Grandma replied with a big smile. "Now let's open them and see if you can tell us a story."

Each egg was numbered, so Jesse opened Egg #1. Inside was a long green leaf.

"It's a piece of palm, just like in the Bible," Jesse explained. "When the people heard that Jesus was coming to town, they got excited. Everyone had heard of the great things Jesus was doing, healing the sick and even raising the dead. They called Him the new coming King. Some people didn't know His kingdom was in Heaven. They thought Jesus was coming to save them from all their problems here

on earth. When Jesus rode into the city of Jerusalem on a donkey, some people spread big leafy branches on the road for Him and others waved them saying 'Hosanna in the Highest!'"

"That's right Jesse," Grandma said. "And these are the same kind of palms we get in church on Palm Sunday."

"Lets open Egg #2." Inside were three shiny dimes.

"Three dimes?" Jesse questioned.

"I'll give you a clue," said Grandma. "Three dimes equal 30 cents. What are dimes made of?"

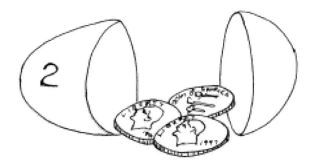

"Silver!" Jesse exclaimed. "I get it. Thirty pieces of silver! That is the price Judas was paid for telling the chief priests and rulers where and when they could find Jesus away from the crowds of people. They were jealous of Jesus. They told Judas that they only wanted to talk to Jesus. Judas had a heart like a tax collector; they heard he loved money. But they didn't tell Judas that they were going to kill Jesus."

"I think you are catching on Jesse," M♡m said. "Now open Egg #3." Inside was a piece of cracker and a tiny bottle.

"This tells the story about the Last Supper. Jesus ate with His friends. They are called disciples," Jesse went on to explain, "twelve men who followed Jesus. He was their teacher. Jesus told them to take the bread and eat and drink the wine. 'This is my body and blood which will be given up for you so that your sins would be forgiven. Do it often to remember me when I am gone.' That is why we still take communion at church today."

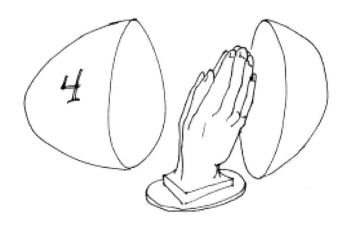

Then Jesse opened Egg #4. Inside was a little pair of hands folded in prayer.

"This means we are to pray to Jesus," Jesse said.

"Yes, but do you remember what happened after Jesus and His disciples were done with their supper?" Grandma asked.

"Oh, yeah! That's when Jesus went into the garden to pray to His Father, God, for strength," Jesse said. "Jesus knew what was going to happen. He was afraid. The Bible says, in Luke 22:44, that He even sweated drops of blood. While He prayed, His friends fell asleep. Then the soldiers came to get Him."

"Slow down Jesse," M♡m said. "Open Egg #5."

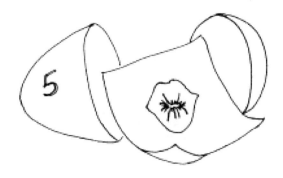

Inside was a piece of paper with a mark that looked like a kiss or a pair of lips.

"The soldiers didn't know which man was Jesus. They didn't have newspapers and TV back in those days, and not everyone knew what Jesus looked like. So when Judas came over and kissed Jesus on the cheek, that was the secret signal. Now the soldiers knew which man to arrest." Jesse opened Egg #6 and out fell a tiny sword and what looked like an ear.

"I know what this means!" Jesse exclaimed. "One of Jesus' disciples tried to stop the soldiers from taking Jesus away. He grabbed his sword and cut off one of the man's ears. But Jesus said, 'Stop! No more of this,' and He picked up the man's ear and healed him."

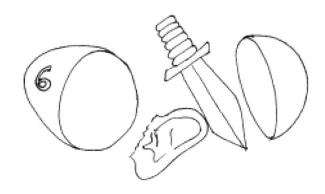

"Go on Jesse," M♡m said. "Open another egg; you're doing a great job of telling the story."

Jesse opened Egg #7.

"A piece of rope, just like they used to tie Jesus' hands and take him to jail. It could also be part of the whip used to beat Jesus on the back.

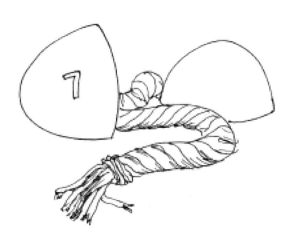

That one was easy." When Jesse opened Egg #8, out came a small toy chicken.

"A chicken?" Jesse said with surprise.

"No, it's a rooster," M♡m answered. "Remember the rooster that crowed two times?"

"Yes," Jesse said. "Jesus told Peter at the Last Supper, 'Before the night is over you will say you don't know me three times.' Peter said he wouldn't. But after they arrested Jesus, people recognized Peter. He was afraid of being arrested too, so he lied and said he didn't know Jesus. When the rooster crowed, Peter realized what he had done and was ashamed."

"That's right, Jesse." Grandma added. "Jesus also said in Matthew 10:32-33, 'If you pretend you don't know me here on earth in front of others, I'll say I don't know you in front of my Father, God in Heaven!'"

"I don't think I would ever do that," Jesse added.

"I would hope not Jesse. However, Peter walked daily with Jesus and saw all those miracles, and he still denied Him. Would we have more faith today than Peter had back then?" M♡m asked.

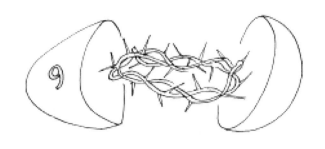

Jesse got real quiet for a minute and said, "Well, maybe I would be afraid like Peter."

M♡m opened Egg #9. Inside was a tiny circle of thorns from a rose bush or a berry bush. Jesse reached in and took it out carefully so as not to get pinched. "This looks like the crown of thorns the soldiers put on Jesus' head, only His was much bigger and sharper. Ouch," Jesse yelled, "that hurts and look, I'm bleeding!"

"You'll be ok. It's only one drop of blood. But just imagine how much the real crown of thorns must have hurt and how much more blood there was," M♡m added.

While M♡m put a band-aid on Jesse's finger, Grandma opened Egg #10. Inside was a small wooden cross and three nails.

"Wow," Jesse said. "Just think how big the real cross must have been and how heavy it was to carry up the hill to Calvary."

"Yes," M♡m added. "Remember it had to be big and strong enough to hold the weight of Jesus' body after they pounded the big nails into his hands and feet to hold Him up there. Looking at these small things makes us forget how terrible it must have been using the real things." M♡m opened Egg #11. "A pair of dice and a piece of purple cloth. Do you know this one Jesse?" She asked.

"Yes, I do," Jesse answered. "After they put Jesus on the cross, the soldiers all wanted his robe. It was made of one piece of fine cloth, so they decided to cast lots for it. Lots are like the game of dice in the olden days. There He was dying on the cross, and those guys only cared about getting His clothes.

"Remember, Jesse, those men didn't believe Jesus was the Son of God. They were following the king's orders, and why not use His clothes? After all, He would never wear them again. People were killed that way everyday for crimes. They didn't know Jesus was special," Grandma added.

Jesse opened Egg #12. Out popped a piece of sponge with a toothpick in it.

"I'm not sure what this is," Jesse said.

"I'll give you a clue," M♡m replied. "While hanging on the cross someone saw that Jesus was trying to speak. One of them dipped a…"

"I know now," Jesse added. "He dipped the sponge into sour wine and held it up on a stick for Jesus to drink, and He did. But He didn't drink it the first time they offered it to Him."

"That's right, Jesse, and in Matthew 27 verse 34, our Bible tells us that before putting Jesus on the cross they offered Him sour wine mixed with an herb called gall. It was a kind of painkiller, but Jesus refused. He knew He had to bear all the pain to have our sins forgiven," Grandma explained.

"Now, let's open Egg #13."

"It's a piece of white linen cloth like they wrapped Jesus in before they put Him in the grave," Jesse said. "That was an easy one too."

When Jesse opened Egg #14, out fell a small flat stone.

"I know this one too. In the olden days graves were dug into the side of hills, like caves. To cover the opening they used big boulders or rocks. This would keep animals from digging up dead people and robbers from stealing out of the graves. It would take two to three men to move one of those big stones."

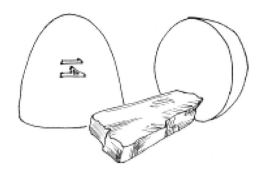

"That's right," said Grandma, "and what did Jesus say would happen on the third day?"

"I know that answer too!" Jesse replied. "Mary the M♡ther of Jesus and the other Mary, went to the grave and found that someone had moved the stone away."

"Stop there, Jesse, and open Egg #15," said M♡m.

When Jesse opened the egg, he said in surprise, "It's empty!"

"Yes, that is just what the women said. The tomb was empty! Jesus had risen! The Bible tells us that Jesus walked on this earth for 40 more days. Many people saw Him, touched Him, and even ate dinner with Him." Grandma continued, "Many thought He would be here forever. Then Jesus told them that He was going to prepare a place for them in His Father's House. He told His followers to wait and pray. He would send them a helper after He was gone.

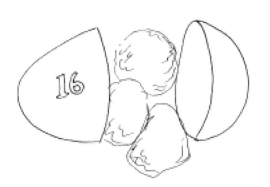

"Now open Egg #16."

When Jesse did, three fluffy cotton balls drifted to the floor. Jesse looked puzzled as he reached down to pick them up.

M♡m said to him, "Use your imagination and think. Where did Jesus go after He told them to wait for the helper?"

"He went to Heaven. Oh, I get it. These are the clouds!" They all started to giggle. "This is fun. I can't wait to show my friends," Jesse said.

"There is still one egg left, Jesse. Open it," M♡m said. When he opened Egg #17, inside was a small white bird.

Jesse said, "It's a dove! The same symbol used in the Bible for the Holy Spirit. That's the helper Jesus told them to wait and pray for. Only this time it is in the form of tongues of fire above each person's head."

"Yes, and we have that same helper, that voice inside, that guides us in choosing right from wrong when we have Jesus living in our hearts as our Savior," Grandma explained.

"Grandma, can I take these eggs to Sunday school?" Jesse asked.

"Sure, they are yours to keep and share with everyone," she replied.

"I have a better idea," M♡mmy added. "Why don't we make another set for your teacher, Mrs. Eichhorn, to keep and one for your cousin Chelsea. That's what Grandma and I did for my friends after I got my set of Easter Eggs."

"That's a great idea M♡m! Could we really?" Jesse said in excitement.

"Sure," M♡m replied. "It's a fun way of sharing the true meaning of Easter. Who knows, Jesse? This could help introduce an unsaved friend to Jesus."

"Hey M♡m, I know something we could put into Egg #18."

"What's that Jesse?" She asked.

"A tiny Bible. Jesus told us to go out into the world and give his message to everyone, and it's all written in the Bible."

"That's a wonderful idea, Jesse, let's get started."

Mom got out a paper and started to make a list of supplies they would need.

Jesse looked up at Grandma. "You know, you're a lot like my Bible."

"I am?" replied Grandma. "In what way?" she asked, looking puzzled.

"Well, you've been around for a long time. You're full of wisdom and good things. You're always talking about Jesus and how to get to Heaven. The more I get to know about you the more I love you too!"

"Oh, thank you Jesse. I think that's the nicest thing anyone has ever said to me." Then Grandma gave Jesse a great big hug.

The Two Princesses

Dian Layton
Illustrated by Al Berg

I n the Kingdom of Human Heart there lived two princesses and they were sisters.

Their names were Quiet and Gentle Spirit, and Selfish Desire.

Selfish Desire was a beautiful girl with shining hair and long flowing gowns...but unfortunately, she had a self-centered and very stubborn heart. Her greatest longing was to fill every day doing things to make herself happier. She spent hours sitting in front of her mirror, eating dainty foods, and commanding the castle servants to wait on her.

Quiet and Gentle Spirit was very different from her sister. Although she too was beautiful to look at, her real beauty was in her peaceful countenance and gentle

ways. Her greatest desire was to fill every day doing things that would make other people happy.

She loved to sing for the village children. She loved to visit people in the prison and hospital. And she loved to help the cooks in the castle kitchen—peeling potatoes, icing cakes, and…sampling soups!

Quiet and Gentle Spirit was loved by the Kingdom.

Beyond the sea, in a magnificent palace, lived the Great King. From time to time, the king would send His Messenger into the Kingdom of Human Heart. And it came to pass on a certain day that the Messenger arrived once again in the Kingdom, riding a white horse. When He blew the golden trumpet, and opened the

Royal Scroll, a crowd gathered quickly. Then the Messenger lifted his voice, and began to read:

"Hear ye, hear ye, hear ye! All young maidens and princesses are to prepare themselves, for the King's only Son—the Prince—is coming to choose a Bride. And behold, He is coming quickly!"

As the Messenger galloped away, the whole kingdom of Human Heart stirred with excitement! The Prince was coming to choose a Bride! All of the young maidens and princesses hurried to the village to get their hair done and buy new dresses…and Quiet and Gentle Spirit and Selfish Desire were just as excited as the rest.

"Just think—the Prince is coming! The Prince is coming!"

As the two Princesses hurried down the road to the village, suddenly their attention was caught by a pitiful groaning noise. They ran over to a ditch, where they saw a tattered looking old man lying in a crumpled heap, loudly complaining of hunger and thirst. At the sight of such a wretch, Selfish Desire held her nose, sneered, and hurried on her way.

But Quiet and Gentle Spirit rushed to his side. "You poor man!" she cried, as he struggled to his feet. "Here, let me help you! I'll take you to the castle and have the cooks fix you a meal fit for a king! And we'll get some new clothes for you too! Now, don't you worry about a thing!" And off they went to the castle.

The old man ate and drank until he fell into a peaceful sleep beside the fire. Quiet and Gentle Spirit laughed happily, then hurried once again toward the village. "Just think! The Prince is coming! I wonder what He looks like!"

She was just approaching the village when she heard someone crying. There beside the road sat a young man, sobbing loudly. Quiet and Gentle Spirit sat down beside him, gave him a handkerchief, and patted his shoulder. "What's wrong?" she asked softly.

"Well I...I...I'm new around here, and I d...d...don't know anyone, and I d....d...don't have any m...m...money...and...and...it will be d...d...dark soon, and...and..." The stranger's voice dropped to a whisper. He paused, and looked into her eyes for a moment, as though he were trying to see if she could be trusted, "...and I m...m...miss my...t...teddy-bear!"

"There, there," said the princess soothingly. "We have plenty of extra room in the castle! You can stay in the royal guest room tonight, and I'll make sure that a coach takes you safely home in the morning." Then she hugged him close and whispered, "And I have an extra teddy-bear you can have to keep!"

By the time the stranger had eaten a good supper, been tucked in for the night with his new teddy-bear, and every tear had disappeared from his eyes, it was too late to go shopping. The stores in the village had closed for the night. The princess sat at her window thoughtfully. There would still be time. In the morning she would

rush down to the village and buy the prettiest dress you could find, and have her hair done in beautiful curls...

Quiet and Gentle Spirit fell asleep wondering what the Prince looked like and dreaming about the great Palace beyond the Sea.

In the morning, as the sun rose and the rooster crowed, Quiet and Gentle Spirit jumped out of bed. She must hurry! The Messenger said the Prince was coming quickly!

But a sudden realization flooded her heart. Oh no! How could she have forgotten?

Today was the day of the week that she visited people in the prison and hospital. They would be expecting her—she couldn't disappoint them!

Oh well. If she hurried, surely there would still be time for the new dress and curls!

And the princess ran to the kitchen to get the chocolate-chip cookies she had made the day before.

That morning at the prison, one new prisoner was especially in need of Quiet and Gentle Spirit's visit. He was grumbly and miserable and ornery! But the princess fed him cookies, sang songs, and told him that he needed a better attitude—he needed to have a dream in his heart! And as he munched the cookies, the prisoner began looking at his circumstances in a different way. "Yeah...she's right! I do need to have a better attitude!" He thanked the princess again and again for her visit. Quiet and Gentle Spirit sighed happily, waved goodbye, and hurried off to the meadow to pick flowers for her friends in the hospital.

When she reached the hospital, the princess met a very sick man. He said that his head hurt, his throat was sore, his stomach was upset, and even his little toe was aching. The princess patted his hand, and quietly put some flowers in a vase

beside the window. While she read words from the Great Book, the man rested peacefully and began to feel much better. Quiet and Gentle Spirit was sitting beside the hospital bed, looking into his eyes, when suddenly she remembered the Prince. Oh no! She had spent far too much time here! The Messenger had said quickly!

The princess knew she must hurry. Down the road she ran, her hair tangling in the wind and her dress becoming increasingly tattered and dusty—but soon she reached the village. "Now, let's see—this won't take long." But as soon as she put her hand on the latch of the door to the first shop, a piercing call filled the air. It was the messenger's trumpet…

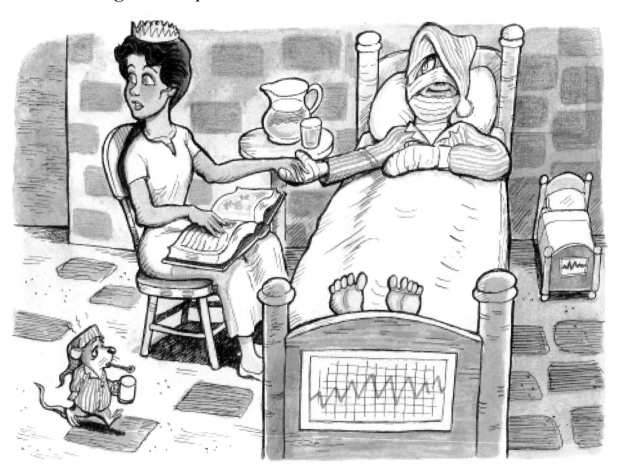

"Hear ye, hear ye, hear ye! All young maidens and princesses are to appear immediately in the castle ballroom...the Prince...has come!"

Quiet and Gentle Spirit turned from the door in shock. "The Prince? No! He can't be here yet! I'm not ready! I'm not ready!" She looked at her dress, and put a hand to her tangled hair. Unbelieving tears welled up in her eyes. "I'm...not...ready."

Time seemed to stand still. All of her dreams of the Prince raced through her mind, then slowly shattered to the bottom of her heart.

"Oh well...I did what I knew was right. I'm really glad I helped all those people. Oh, well...He probably wouldn't have chosen me, anyway. Maybe he will choose Selfish Desire as his bride! She's so pretty...but I wish I could at least see what he looks like."

Hey, why not?!

"I'll just sneak in, and hide in the background! No one will notice me, and I'll be able to see the Prince. I'll be able to see what He looks like."

And off she ran to the castle.

The ballroom was ringing with music, excitement, and nervous giggles when Quiet and Gentle Spirit tip-toed in and peeked out from behind one of the great pillars. Beautiful maidens and princesses, all clothed in lovely gowns and with their hair in shining curls, stood on either side of a long carpeted aisle.

Right at the front of the line was Selfish Desire. She was admiring herself in a mirror, when suddenly she turned and looked right at her sister!

Quiet and Gentle Spirit self-consciously patted her tangled hair and rumbled dress under the disgusted glance. "Oh well..." And then she looked past Selfish Desire, toward the platform.

There, in His magnificent robes, stood the Prince. Quiet and Gentle Spirit looked at the Prince...and she looked at him. There was something about his face...something about His eyes...but wait! He was smiling! He had seen her! Oh no!

And then, at the signal of the Messenger, a hush fell upon the room. Every eye watched in anticipation as the Prince began to walk down the carpeted aisle. The maidens and princesses curtsied and giggled nervously as He passed. Selfish Desire smiled radiantly as He passed, but the Prince didn't even glance her way. He was looking steadily toward a pillar at the end of the room, at a princess with a tattered dress and a crown sitting crooked on her head—with her eyes locked on His.

As the Prince reached her, the others watched in amazement and the silence deepened. Was He going to reprove her for daring to come into His presence in such a manner? Very tenderly, the Prince drew Quiet and Gentle Spirit out from the shadows, and she knelt before Him.

And then, to the shock of the crowd, and to the wonder of the princess, He took her hands, lifted her to her feet, and He knelt in front of her. And the prince began to sing:

> *Oh, Quiet and Gentle Spirit,*
>
> *You have won my heart,*
>
> *Oh, Quiet and Gentle Spirit,*
>
> *You have won my love,*
>
> *I was hungry, and you fed me—*
>
> *I was thirsty—you gave me drink;*
>
> *I was a stranger, and you cared for me…*
>
> *I was sick, and in prison—*
>
> *And you came to me…*
>
> *Oh Quiet and Gentle Spirit,*
>
> *My love is great toward thee,*
>
> *In as much as ye have done it*
>
> *To the least of these*
>
> *You have done it—unto me.*

As he sang, understanding crept into her heart. His eyes! Of course! The old man in the ditch, the stranger by the road, the prisoner, the man in the hospital— all had been the prince! Slowly, He stood to His feet, and turned to the astonished crowd, and to the very astonished Selfish Desire.

And His words echoed throughout the Kingdom of Human Heart.

Selfish Desire, you must change

your heart, your ways, your very name—

to be self-less,

and not selfish…

Then true happiness will come your way.

The prince touched Quiet and Gentle Spirit, and in one miraculous moment, in the twinkling of an eye, she was changed. All the beauty within her appeared for everyone to see. She was clothed in a radiant white wedding gown. Her hair became a mass of lovely curls, and the Prince put a glittering new crown upon her head.

Then the Prince took Quiet and Gentle Spirit home to His Father's kingdom, where they ruled and reigned together forever, and ever, and ever.

The Lady and Her City

Dian Layton
Illustrated by Al Berg

Once upon a real time there lived a Lady who had her very own city.

That sounds exciting…but it wasn't.

You see, her city was a terrible place to live.

The walls that surrounded it were broken down.

The buildings were falling apart.

The streets were filled with garbage.

Everywhere she turned it was very, very dark.

And in her city lived many horrible characters—

Some of the worst were called Fear, Guilt, Pain, and Bitterness.

The Lady longed to leave her city, and move to a nice new home, but she couldn't.

The city belonged to her—it was the only place she had, and she couldn't leave it.

Sometimes she would try to clean things up a bit, but it seemed that the harder she tried, the dirtier things became.

Sometimes she tried to get rid of the horrible characters who wandered her streets, but they would only build new houses, and invite more of their relatives to move in.

The Lady became very discouraged.

One day, she was standing at the city gate, looking out at the world around her and wondering what to do.

Suddenly, she saw someone walking toward her.

It was the King!

She had heard about him, but had never seen him before.

The King came to the gate.

The Lady knelt in front of him, and the King reached out his hands and helped her to her feet.

He spoke soft, kind words like the Lady had never heard before.

He told her that He wanted to give her a new life; He wanted to fill her city with His light, and move her to a hill for everyone to see.

The King asked the lady to give her city to Him.

It was not a hard decision.

She knew she hadn't done a very good job of running things on her own.

The Lady invited the King to take over her city.

As soon as He walked in, there were many changes.

Light spread down the streets and into some of the buildings.

Fear, Guilt, Pain, and Bitterness covered their eyes and went shrieking out of the city, followed by every other terrible character who had been living there.

The Lady looked at the King in amazement.

What a difference He had made already!

The King introduced her to two new friends.

Their names were Joy and Peace.

The Lady had never known anyone like them.

They were so bright, and so confident, that as they took her hands in theirs, the Lady actually felt joy and peace fill her heart.

Then the King gave her a letter.

He told her to read from it every day.

He said that it would tell her how to spread His light into every part of her city.

It would give instructions for cleaning and repairing the walls, streets and buildings.

Joy and Peace would help her; and the King promised to always be near, even though she couldn't see Him.

He told her to spend time with Him every day.

All she had to do was close her eyes, and speak—He would hear her.

The Lady decided to try. She closed her eyes and imagined His face...

When she opened her eyes, He was gone.

But somehow, the Lady knew He was watching her.

She got to work right away.

It was so exciting!

The King's letter was like reading a Book of Life, and speaking to Him each day made her feel strong and happy.

Joy and Peace became her best friends, as together they built up her walls and repaired the city.

Everything would have been wonderful, except for one thing.

The Lady had an enemy.

The enemy hated her, and he hated the King.

He decided to do everything in his power to destroy her city.

And so it was that one day, just as the Lady was putting the finishing touches on the gate, she looked up in amazement.

The enemy was coming down the road toward her!

And he wasn't alone.

Fear, Guilt, Pain, and Bitterness were close behind him.

Quickly she locked the gate, and called out loudly,

"Get away from here! You have no right to come near here!

This city belongs to the King!"

At the sound of her voice, the enemy stopped in his tracks.

His ugly companions looked around and whined fearfully at the mention of the King.

They all huddled and whispered together, then turned and walked away.

As she watched them leave, the lady felt Joy and Peace move closer.

"Whew!" she said, "That was scary! I think my walls and gates are strong enough if they try to attack, but I had better put guards around."

Joy and Peace agreed, and her guard was set up.

Some of those who went on duty were Patience and Perseverance.

The Lady chose Understanding and Caution to stand by the gate.

Every day, the Lady read the King's letter and spent time talking with Him.

As she worked with Joy and Peace, the city became a fortress,

and little by little, light was filling every part.

Then, one day, someone new entered the city.

Perhaps a window had been left open somewhere,

or one of the guards wasn't watching closely enough.

The visitor looked harmless.

He was small and wore a gray cloak.

His name was Little Doubt.

He spoke softly to the Lady, and she listened to his voice.

She noticed that Joy and Peace didn't like him—

but she felt certain that it would be all right to let him stay,

just for awhile.

After all…he was only a…Little Doubt…

The next day, Little Doubt was joined by Little Worry.

He too, was small and dressed in a gray cloak.

He too, seemed quite harmless.

In fact, the Lady quite enjoyed their company.

They were cute, and little,

and they seemed very concerned about her well-being.

They sat with her and asked her many interesting questions.

"What if…?" and "Have you ever thought of…?" and "Do you really know…?"

During the next days, many Little Doubts and Little Worries roamed the city streets, and the Lady often took time from her work to listen to their voices.

"You have been working so hard." "Is it really worth it?"

"How can you be sure that the King will even keep his promise to you?"

Gradually, Joy and Peace became more and more distant,

but the Lady didn't even notice.

One morning, as the Lady sat with all the Doubts and Worries,

a new visitor entered the city.

She was pale, and weak, but strangely beautiful.

Her name was Apathy.

Apathy spoke quietly to the Lady.

"You have been working so hard…you are tired…Come, take a little rest…"

As the Lady yawned and nodded, Apathy continued, "And about the guard that you have put up around the city walls…

That isn't necessary…After all, the King will protect you…"

The Lady nodded again, and let down her guard.

Apathy lead her to a couch and fluffed the pillows invitingly.

The Lady yawned, set the King's letter on a shelf, and lay down on the couch.

And there, with the Little Doubts and Worries patting her hands, and Apathy humming a lullaby, the lady…fell…asleep…

How long did she sleep—a few hours, a few days, a few months?

Perhaps it was even years, but finally, one day, the Lady woke up.

And what she saw when she opened her eyes was terrible.

While she had slept, the enemy had taken over her city.

Darkness surrounded her; the Little Doubts and Worries had grown into towering giants.

Fear, Guilt, Pain, and Bitterness had returned—now stronger than ever before.

The Lady sat up and cried out loudly, "Get out of here, all of you!

You have no right to be here! This city belongs to the King!"

Her enemies laughed and mocked her.

"No right?! But you were the one who let us in!"

"I didn't mean to!" the Lady cried, then looked around frantically,

"Where are Joy and Peace?"

The enemies shrugged their shoulders and laughed again, "Oh dear, she's lost her Joy and Peace."

As Fear gripped her, the Lady jumped to her feet and reached for the King's letter.

She blew the dust off and tried to read it, but the words seemed jumbled and confused.

She closed her eyes and tried to picture the King, but it was too hard.

She was filled with a horrible panic and ran out into the streets.

Every direction she turned was covered with a smothering darkness, and as she ran, the Lady soon realized that she was lost within her own city.

The giants Doubt, Worry, and Fear reached her first and began to wrap her in heavy chains.

Soon, Guilt, Pain, and Bitterness joined them.

The Lady fell to her knees and called out in desperation,
"King! King, please help me! I'm sorry for listening to the Doubts and Worries!
I'm sorry for falling asleep! Forgive me, King! Help me, help me!"

Immediately the enemies stopped their torment and looked around anxiously.

Everyone waited silently for several moments…

But nothing happened.

Nothing…happened.

The enemies were relieved, and pulled the chains tighter.

Bitterness laughed, "See? He doesn't hear you anymore!"

Guilt's voice pushed in loudly, "It's all your fault…you let it happen…"

"Now it's too late…too late…" Worry and Doubt echoed.

Then, in the distance, they heard footsteps.

Someone was running toward them—closer…closer…

Through the darkness came a little girl.

She hurried to the Lady, threw her arms around her, and hugged her tightly.

"Hi!" she said happily. "My name is Hope.

The King has heard your cry, and he sent me with a message.

It is one word: Rejoice!"

The Lady shook her head in unbelief.

"Rejoice?!" she whispered.

"You want me to rejoice?!

In the middle of this darkness…with all my Fears and Doubts and Worries…

you want me to…rejoice?"

Hope hugged the Lady even more tightly and nodded. "Rejoice."

For a few moments the Lady was silent; then she smiled weakly.

"Well, the King did hear my cry. He did send a…little Hope.

All right. I…will…rejoice."

Immediately her enemies lost some of their power, and the chains loosened.

The Lady stood to her feet and shut her eyes tightly to their faces.

"I don't care how dark it is.

I don't care how big my Fears and Doubts and Worries are; It doesn't matter how many problems and troubles I have.

I…will…rejoice!"

The Lady lifted her hands and began to sing a song of praise to the King.

As she sang, her enemies became smaller and smaller, and light began to return to the city.

Joy and Peace came and joined her song.

The Lady's voice was weak and trembling at first, but gradually it became stronger, until she was singing so loudly that her enemies were cowering and crying out in pain.

Then the Lady took the now Little Fears, Doubts, Worries, Guilt, and Bitterness—and threw them out of the City.

The enemy would not give up. He would attack again.

But next time he would meet a well-guarded city, and a Lady embracing the King's letter to her heart.

OTHER BOOKS SOLD SEPARATELY:

Adventures in the Kingdom Series

Harold and I Series

Hinds' Feet Illustrated

Mommy, Why Did Jesus Have to Die?

Mommy, Why Can't I Watch That TV Show?

Mommy, Why Don't We Celebrate Halloween?

Mommy, Why Are People Different Colors?

Mommy, Was Santa Born on Christmas Too?

Mommy, Why Do We Have Easter?
(with full color illustrations inside)

Seeker

Soldiers with Little Feet

Made in United States
North Haven, CT
01 December 2023